The Saints' Guide to
HELP WHEN LIFE HURTS

The Saints' Guide to
HELP WHEN LIFE HURTS

Cynthia Cavnar

SERVANT PUBLICATIONS
ANN ARBOR, MICHIGAN

Charis Books is an imprint of Servant Publications especially designed to serve Roman Catholics.

Published by Servant Publications
P.O. Box 8617
Ann Arbor, Michigan 48107

Cover design by Paul Higdon - Minneapolis, MN

01 02 03 10 9 8 7 6 5 4 3 2 1

Printed in the United States of America
ISBN 0-56955-234-7

Library of Congress Cataloging-in-Publication Data

Cavnar, Cindy.
The saints' guide to help when life hurts / Cynthia Cavnar.
p cm.
ISBN 1-56955-234-7 (alk. paper)
1. Christian saints—Biography. 2. Christian saints—Meditations. I. Title.

BX4651.2 .C38 2001
242'4.—dc21

2001028742

CONTENTS

INTRODUCTION

A friend of mine teaches theology to high school students. One day, as she presented a lesson on the Holy Spirit, she felt particularly inspired by the material. The words flowed, her enthusiasm mounted, and she even managed to ignore the student sitting in the front row, insistently raising her hand. But the young woman wouldn't give up. Finally my friend called on her.

"Ms. Brown," the student said plaintively, "are you talking to us?"

So much for inspiration. As my friend learned, no amount of insight on one side makes up for lack of comprehension on the other.

And so it is with the question of suffering. The Christian approach to the subject baffles many of those outside the faith (and sometimes those within). The nonbeliever sees the horror of suffering, especially of the innocent, and can't find any good in it. Christians see the horror as well but also recognize that it was through suffering that God chose to bring about the redemption of the world, in the passion and death of Jesus on the cross.

Nevertheless, as Pope John Paul II points out in his letter *Salvifici Dolores* ("On the Christian Meaning of Human Suffering"), "the meaning of suffering ... always remains a mystery." Some suffering is a result of sin, he says, but not all. As if to underline humanity's inability to finally nail the topic down, he adds: "We are conscious of the insufficiency and inadequacy of our explanations."

Still, the saints have plenty to say about the topic. Not all of it is helpful. In an earlier age, saints sometimes indulged in an excess of self-inflicted pain in reparation for their sins. They whipped themselves till the blood ran, and they fasted to the extreme. The church today, while encouraging penance, rejects penitential extremes. In fact, it has always had many saints who failed to see much good in those practices. St. Basil questioned the strict fasting of his early days, blaming it for his later frail health. One of the most beloved saints of modern times, Thérèse of Lisieux, found the little trials and humiliations of daily life crucifying enough: "The only mortification granted me was to master my self-love, and that did me far more good than any bodily penance."

Self-imposed pain aside, suffering is an inevitable part of human existence. It goes well beyond the burden of sickness and death to include the sometimes more devastating pain of loneliness, loss of faith, depression, abandonment, mental illness, and other traumas of the spirit. It is not good in and of itself: "Let it be understood that [pain] has no sanctifying influence in itself," Cardinal Newman said. "Bad men are made worse by it." All the saints agree, however, that sufferings endured in imitation of Christ can have a transforming effect. Essentially, suffering can help the Christian die to self and become more like Christ.

The saints expect such suffering to enlarge the spirit rather than confine it and to turn the Christian outward in service to others rather than inward in self-absorbed grief. In fact, easing the suffering of others, even if we are suffering ourselves, is a constant theme in the writings of the saints. Such assistance should "not stop at sympathy and compassion alone," Pope John Paul II says in *Salvifici Dolores,* but should be "as far as possible effective."

Not surprisingly, many of the saints made their mark through direct works of mercy: feeding the poor, nursing the sick, building hospitals and orphanages. If you are at prayer and the poor come for assistance, St. Vincent de Paul said in a remarkable statement, "leave God for God." Perhaps because they suffered so much themselves, the saints always seemed ready to listen to, console, encourage, pray for, and generally make themselves available to the suffering.

As we see throughout this book, the saints offer many tips on coping with pain of mind and body. On the other hand, they insist on a fundamental truth: No Christian escapes the cross. "Are you forgetting the words of our Savior?" St. John Vianney asked. "'If anyone will come after me, let him deny himself and take up his cross daily and follow me.'"

ONE

IN THE SHADOW OF THE CROSS

On August 9, 1945, American forces dropped an atomic bomb over Nagasaki, Japan. Nearly seventy-four thousand people died immediately; another eighty thousand died later from the effects of radiation. The bomb exploded directly over the Catholic quarter of the city, incinerating hundreds of Catholic grade school children who were gathered in the cathedral for confession prior to the Feast of the Assumption.

One of those who survived the blast was a Catholic doctor, Takashi Nagai, dean of the radiology department at the Nagasaki University Medical School. In the aftermath of the explosion, he said, "everything outside grew dark. There was a noise like the sound of a stormy sea, and the air everywhere swirled.... Then it gradually became cold as at the end of autumn, and a strange and silent emptiness ensued."

Ignoring his own injuries, Dr. Nagai organized medical students to help other survivors. But "we were helpless and empty-handed. We had no medicines, no instruments, no bandages." Two days later he managed to get to his own home. There he found the burned bones of his wife, her hand still grasping a rosary and crucifix.

In the middle of this "great cry of human pain," as he called it, Dr. Nagai drew on his faith to sustain him. In particular, he saw the circumstances as an opportunity to do reparation for sin: "We must now walk along a path that is full of human pain and suffering and, as we walk, ... let us remember how Jesus Christ carried his cross to the hill of Calvary."

Nagai built a little hut to live in and called it "The House of Loving Others as Thyself." "We have forgotten that we are children of God," he said. "We have believed in idols; we have destroyed the law of love. We have joyfully hated one another. We have joyfully killed one another."

Nagai lived six more years before dying of leukemia. During that time, although he was in pain and often bedridden, he became an outspoken advocate of reconciliation and peace. The Japanese parliament named him a national hero.

The theologian Karl Barth once said of the Christian attitude toward suffering: "Our tribulation, without ceasing to be tribulation, is transformed." Dr. Nagai's life makes the same point. He endured one of the most terrible moments of history but lived to prove that there is hope even in the middle of unimaginable suffering. All the quotes that follow—from those describing the need to carry the crosses we are given to those highlighting the various virtues (such as patience) that will help us do so—lead in the same direction.

The Problem of Suffering

Blessed Henry Suso, a fourteenth-century mystic, sometimes expressed himself in memorable imagery: "God is the circle whose center is everywhere but whose circumference is nowhere," he wrote in his autobiography. But he could also be plainspoken, as is evident in his devotional work *The Little Book of Eternal Wisdom.* In this, one of the most popular religious works of the late Middle Ages, Suso referred to Christ as "the Eternal Wisdom" and to himself as "the servant of the Eternal Wisdom." In the following dialogue Suso poses questions that have troubled Christians in every age.

The Servant: Lord, I have something on my heart. May I tell you about it? May I dispute with you like holy Jeremiah? Lord, this is what people say: However sweet your love might be, you allow it to prove very harsh to your friends. You send them many severe trials such as the scorn of the world and both inward and outward sufferings. They say that scarcely do people become your friends than they have to gather up their courage for suffering. Lord, by your goodness, what sweetness can they have in this? How can you allow this to happen to your friends? Or are you pleased to know nothing about it?

Eternal Wisdom: Even as the Father loves me, so I love my friends. I treat my friends now the same way that I've treated them from the beginning of the world.

Servant: That's what they complain about. They say that therefore you have very few friends because you barely allow them to prosper in this world. For the same reason, many who become your friends and ought to remain faithful in suffering, fall away from you. Woe is me! I say with sorrow and bitter tears that they relapse into the state which, through you, they had forsaken. Lord, what do you have to say about that?

Eternal Wisdom: This is the complaint of people of weak faith and small works, of a lukewarm life and undisciplined spirit. But you, beloved soul, get your mind out of the slime and slough of carnal pleasures! Unlock your interior sense, open your spiritual eyes and see.... You will understand that I do the very best for my friends.

... Just as a small drop makes little difference in the vast depth of the sea, just so little can the things of this world contribute to the fulfillment of your desires. You are in this wretched valley of tears, where joy and sorrow, laughing and weeping are mingled together. No heart ever attained perfect happiness here, for the world is false and full of deceit, more than I will say. It promises much but delivers little. [Life] is short, uncertain, and changeable; today much joy, tomorrow a heart full of sorrow.

Blessed Henry Suso
Adapted from *The Little Book of Eternal Wisdom*

We are the children of a crucified God.

St. John Vianney
Sermons

Like the Master

Pope John Paul II reminds us that Jesus, too, was a man of suffering and stands in solidarity with those who suffer.

God is always on the side of the suffering. His omnipotence is manifested precisely in the fact that he freely accepted suffering. He could have chosen not to do so. He could have chosen to demonstrate his omnipotence even at the moment of the crucifixion. In fact, it was proposed to him: "Let the Messiah, the King of Israel, come down now from the cross that we may see and believe" (Mk 15:32). But he did not accept that challenge. The fact that he stayed on the cross until the end, the fact that on the cross he could say, as do all who suffer, "My God, my God, why have you forsaken me?" (Mk 15:34), has remained in human history *the strongest argument* [that God is on the side of the suffering]. If the agony on the cross had not happened, the truth that God is love would have been unfounded.

Yes! God is love, and precisely for this he gave his Son, to reveal himself completely as love. Christ is the one who *"loved ... to the end"* (Jn 13:1). "To the end" means to the last breath. "To the end" means accepting all the consequences of man's sin, taking it upon himself. This happened exactly as the prophet Isaiah affirmed: "It was our infirmities that he bore.... We had all gone astray like sheep, each following his own way; but the Lord laid upon him the guilt of us all" (Is 53:4-6).

Pope John Paul II
Crossing the Threshold of Hope

> If God created shadows, it was in order to better emphasize the light.
>
> Bl. Pope John XXIII
> *Wit and Wisdom of Good Pope John*

Jesus would have liked to avoid the passion and death that awaited him, had that been possible. In the middle of suffering, and in anticipation of greater suffering yet to come, he chose a higher good—to do the will of the Father. He submitted even when the Father refused his request to allow the cup of suffering to pass him by (Mt 26:39).

> The Father did not take the cup away from his Son. The prayer of Gethsemane, in which a true man was expressing before God all the psychological and existential truth about fear in the face of suffering and death, ends with acceptance of the timeless decision whereby the Father "did not spare his own Son" (Rom 8:32) but made him "become sin for our sake" (2 Cor 5:21)....
>
> We should bear in mind that this true man who, humanly speaking, is now left with his prayer to the Father unanswered, is the same man who at twelve years old had said: "Why did you go searching for me? Did you not know that I must attend to what concerns my Father?" (Lk 2:49). He spoke those words to his mother and Joseph after their three days of troubled and anxious searching. The words of the twelve-year-old now acquire their full value and meaning: now, when he is on his knees in Gethsemane, when the Father makes it clear to him that he must drink to the bitter end the cup which his human nature shudders to contemplate....
>
> We are [now] face-to-face with the inner truth of this man foretold by the prophet Isaiah as the "servant of Yahweh," the truth which shaped the whole of his inner life: "I always do what is pleasing to him" (Jn 8:29).
>
> Pope John Paul II
> *Sign of Contradiction*

> It is not a blessed thing to be in the midst of suffering; but it is blessed to be victorious over it, and not to be cowed by the power of temporal pain.
>
> St. Ambrose
> *Duties of the Clergy*

Pure Love

In meditating on Jesus being taken prisoner in the Garden, two things touched me very much and occupied my thoughts: first, the way Christ went forward to meet those who had come to apprehend him: his firmness, courage and peace just as if his soul had been steeped in calm. His heart is full of anguish, his human nature is disconcerted, yet amidst it all it turns straight to God the Father; it does not hesitate about taking the way suggested by the highest virtue and self-sacrifice.

One of the greatest gifts the Holy Spirit can bestow on us is to give us peace in time of struggle, calm in the midst of trouble, so that in time of desolation we are armed with so virile a courage that nature, the devil, and even God himself, who seems to be against us, cannot withstand.

The second thing that struck me was our Lord's disposition with regard to Judas who betrayed him, the apostles who abandoned him and to the priests and others who were the cause of the persecution he suffered. Amidst it all Jesus remained perfectly calm. His love for his disciples and enemies was not altered at all.... His heart was without

> bitterness and full of tenderness toward his enemies in spite of their perfidy and of all they made him suffer.
>
> St. Claude de la Colombière
> *The Spiritual Direction of Blessed Claude de la Colombière*

In *The Imitation of Christ,* Thomas à Kempis regrets the general absence among Christians of a pure love for Jesus. Most people are unwilling to carry their cross in partnership with him.

> Jesus always has many who love his heavenly kingdom, but few who bear his cross. He has many who desire consolation, but few who care for trial. He finds many to share his table, but few to take part in his fasting. All desire to be happy with him; few wish to suffer anything for him. Many follow him to the breaking of bread, but few to the drinking of the chalice of his passion. Many revere his miracles; few approach the shame of the cross. Many love him as long as they encounter no hardship; many praise and bless him as long as they receive some comfort from him. But if Jesus hides himself and leaves them for awhile, they fall either into complaints or deep dejection.
>
> Those, on the contrary, who love him for his own sake and not for any comfort of their own, bless him in trials and anguish of heart as well as in the bliss of consolation. Even if he should never give them consolation, yet they would continue to praise him and wish always to give him thanks. What power there is in pure love for Jesus—love that is free from self-interest and self-love!
>
> Thomas à Kempis
> *The Imitation of Christ*

Is Suffering Necessary?

The saints all loved the cross and found in it strength and counsel. But you will say to me, is it necessary, then, always to have something to suffer?... Now sickness or poverty, or again scandal or attacks upon your reputation, or possibly loss of money or sickness?

Have you ever had someone falsely blacken your reputation? Have you been the target of insults? Have you been wronged? So much the better! That is a good sign; do not worry, you are on the road that leads to heaven. Do you know when you ought to be really upset?... When you have nothing to endure....

Are you forgetting that at your Baptism you accepted the cross? You must never abandon it until death; it is the key that you will use to open the door of heaven. Are you forgetting the words of our Savior? "If anyone will come after me, let him deny himself and take up his cross daily and follow me." Not for a day, not for a week, not for a year, but all our lives.

St. John Vianney
Adapted from the *Sermons*

There is a saying in Holy Scripture that I think we should always remember. It says that Jerusalem will be rebuilt in *angustia temporum* ["in time of affliction," Dn 9:25]. We have to work in *angustia temporum* all our lives. Our difficulties are not a transitory state of affairs, to be allowed to pass by like a squall of wind, so that we can work on when the weather grows calm. No, they are the normal state of affairs, and we should reckon on being in *angustia temporum* all our lives so far as the good we want to do is concerned.

Venerable Charles de Foucauld
Spiritual Autobiography of Charles de Foucauld

After you have prayed to the Father to console you, if it does not please him to do it, think of it no more, and stiffen your courage to work out your salvation on the cross, as if you were never to descend from it, and as if you would never see the sky of your life clear and serene....

Now he wants you to serve him without relish, without sentiment, with repugnances and convulsions of spirit. This service gives you no satisfaction, but it contents him. It is not to your pleasure, but it is to his.

St. Francis de Sales
Thy Will Be Done

Consolation in the Midst of Suffering

It is surprising to see the progress we make in times of spiritual privation, and when no joy of any kind comes between our souls and God. It is then indeed himself that we love, and not his consolations; and any right we may then do is indeed pure duty. Then when the difficult road is past, and the way becomes easier, we are astonished to see how far we have come, and may pause in peace and near to the heart of God.

Elisabeth Leseur
A Wife's Story

> When we experience no consolations, we serve God for his own sake; when we have them, we run the risk of serving him for our own sake.
>
> St. John Vianney
> *Sermons*

Venerable Francis Libermann recommends a sort of holy indifference to suffering complemented by abandonment to the love of God.

> Woe to me, if I seek to be at ease on this earth, to live honored and esteemed by men!... Remember one thing: this earth shall pass away; the life we lead lasts but an instant. When our flesh will be corrupted in the tomb, it will be perfectly indifferent whether we have led an easy life or not. Our eternity will not be the happier on that account....
>
> A Christian soul, a soul devoted to our Lord and to his glory alone, should reckon ease and uneasiness, honor and contempt, as being void and indifferent. Why should I wish to lead a comfortable life on this earth unless through self-love?
>
> Let us surrender ourselves to the love of Jesus and not to the love of ourselves. If I am overwhelmed with every imaginable evil, during all the time I have to drag along my body on this earth of woes, what does that matter to me, provided I belong to God, and serve him according to his holy love? And to live this life of love, what state is more favorable than that of crosses, privations, pains, and all sorts of afflictions?
>
> Venerable Francis Libermann
> *Life of the Venerable Liebermann*

God's Sustaining Peace

What is this peace, different from that which the world gives? This peace is the one your love gives ... a peace greater than suffering, not a peace without war, but a peace in spite of war, during war, above war, the peace of the soul having, through love, its whole life in heaven and thus enjoying the peace of heaven in spite of everything which may happen on earth around it and against it.

Venerable Charles de Foucauld
Soldier of the Spirit

What toil we must endure, what fatigue, while we are attempting to climb hills and the summits of mountains! What, that we may ascend to heaven! If you consider the promised reward, what you endure is less. Immortality is given to the one who perseveres; everlasting life is offered; the Lord promises his kingdom.

St. Cyprian
Sermons

Elisabeth Leseur viewed suffering as redemptive. She offered hers up for the needs of her husband, who was an atheist, and others. In her diary she often spoke of the importance of bearing suffering with good cheer, a point that can escape us in the heat of trials. She trained herself to remain serene in the middle of a life filled with pain, including her final decline and death from cancer.

O Lord, you have laid your cross on my soul, on my heart, on my body. Of all suffering, you give me that which pierces my heart the most. Help me to carry this cross without bitterness, without falling, without thoughts of self....

My God, let me renew my prayer to you: That for those I love there may be neither sin nor suffering, that your light may shine on them, that their souls may be sanctified by you. To your care I confide them, and to you I abandon myself. For you I will keep the tears my spirit sheds, for others the smiles on my lips; with you alone I will carry the cross, letting nothing be seen but the light of the Transfiguration, the light I once saw, which went out in the darkness of the cross. On Calvary Jesus carried out his work of redemption; it is in suffering that chosen souls can likewise do their work, in privation and humility.

Elisabeth Leseur
Adapted from *A Wife's Story*

Serenity within, and always gentleness and smiles without, amiable when I feel bad-tempered, welcoming when I long for solitude, friendly when I feel weary and irritable.

Elisabeth Leseur
A Wife's Story

The Suffering of the Damned

Many of the saints write about the definitive suffering of an eternity in hell. St. Alphonsus Liguori's reflections are made more poignant by his considering, from the perspective of eternity, the thoughts of the condemned themselves.

> The greatest torment that the damned will have to endure in hell will be themselves ever preying on themselves by remorse: Their worm does not die. Alas! What a cruel worm it will be to Christians who are lost, to think for how very little they have condemned themselves! Have we then, they will say, for such trifling, transitory, and poisonous gratifications, lost heaven and God and condemned ourselves to this prison of torments forever?
>
> ...At present, what does our past life appear but as a dream, a moment? But what will a life of forty or fifty years appear to the damned when, after hundreds and thousands and millions of years have passed away, they will find that their eternity is still to come?
>
> What will those miserable pleasures for which they have sacrificed their salvation appear to them? They will say, "Have we then, for these accursed gratifications, which were scarcely tasted before they were ended, condemned ourselves to burn forever in this furnace of fire, abandoned by all, for all eternity?"
>
> Another subject of remorse will be the thought of the little that they were required to do in order to be saved. They will say, "Had we pardoned those injuries, had we overcome those human respects, had we avoided those

occasions, we should not have been lost."

What would it cost us to avoid those conversations? To deprive ourselves of those accursed gratifications?... Whatever they have cost us, we ought to have been willing to do everything to obtain salvation; but we did not do so, and now there is no remedy for our eternal ruin.

Had we frequented the sacraments, had we not neglected meditation, had we recommended ourselves to God, we should not have fallen into sin. We frequently proposed to do this, but we did it not. We sometimes began a good course, but we soon discontinued it...

O God of my soul! How many times have I promised to love you, and again turned my back upon you? Oh, by that love with which you died for me on the cross, grant me sorrow for my sins, grant me grace to love you, and ever to turn to you in the time of temptation.

St. Alphonsus Liguori

The Great Means of Perfection and of Salvation

TWO

SUFFERING OF THE HEART: BETRAYAL

The psalmist knew the pain of betrayal: "If an enemy had reviled me, I could have borne it.... But you, my other self, my companion and my bosom friend! You, whose comradeship I enjoyed; at whose side I walked in procession in the house of God!" (Ps 55:13, 14-15).

Jesus, more than anyone, has earned the right to complain about the fickleness of human affection. He gave himself freely during his ministry on earth—to the sick, the poor, the outcast, the disciples, his hand-picked band of apostles, and more. When the chips were down, they rewarded him by betraying him (Judas), denying him (Peter), and fleeing (everybody else, with the exception of his mother, a few devoted women, and John).

Even worse, when the actual moment of crucifixion came, God the Father seemed to lose interest. There was no spiritual comfort to ease Jesus' suffering, as is clear from his final plea: "My God, my God, why have you abandoned me?"

It is a hard but sometimes neglected truth that Jesus' relationships offered him virtually no support when he needed it most. His last moments played out in the middle of betrayal, broken friendships, and what felt like divine neglect.

But it didn't have to end this way, at least not in every detail. Jesus himself pointed out one possible change in the script. When Judas led the soldiers into the Garden to seize him, Jesus said: "Day after day, I sat teaching in the temple area yet you did not arrest me" (Mt 26:55). Had they approached him there—in the temple, in broad daylight, in the center of a crowd—presumably his identity would have been obvious. There would have been no need for Judas' kiss of betrayal.

Cold comfort for Jesus, perhaps, and a moot point anyway, but surely not a detail God failed to consider. Human history is littered with tales of betrayal and broken trust. The fact that God himself endured this bitter experience—and handled it by forgiving—is both a consolation and a challenge to the many since who have faced much the same.

At some point in their lives, most of the saints suffered either the active betrayal of colleagues and, in some cases, spouses or, at the very least, the hostility or neglect of friends. Often, broken friendships followed. The words and example of the saints, together with the example of Jesus, provide food for thought for those similarly afflicted.

> When Christ was in the world, he was despised by humanity. In his hour of need, his acquaintances and friends abandoned him to suffer the depths of scorn. He was willing to suffer and be despised; do you dare complain of anything? He had enemies and defamers; do you want everyone to be your friend, your benefactor? How can your patience be rewarded if no adversity test it? How can you be a friend of Christ if you are not willing to suffer any hardship? Suffer with Christ and for Christ if you wish to reign with him.
>
> Thomas à Kempis
> Adapted from *The Imitation of Christ*

Broken Trust

The parades and green beer of St. Patrick's Day would have puzzled the real St. Patrick. Most Catholics are familiar with the bare bones of his story. He himself gave us the outline in his autobiographical *Confessions*—from his abduction in Britain and enslavement in Ireland through his escape and subsequent life as bishop to the Irish. Most are unaware, however, that at some point in his career—the exact date is uncertain—Patrick experienced a betrayal so devastating that it threatened to undermine his faith.

The precise details are unclear, but Patrick tells us that as a young boy, at a time when he "did not believe in the living God nor had I believed, since my infancy," he committed some sin. Shortly before becoming a deacon, "on account of the anxiety in my sorrowful mind," Patrick revealed the matter to his close friend. Years later, when some questions arose as to Patrick's suitability for the ministry in Ireland, this same friend told the sin to others who were in a position to influence the direction of Patrick's life. Worse, this friend had initially championed Patrick's cause when others, perhaps jealous, questioned Patrick's limited education and accused him of accepting gifts in exchange for administering the sacraments.

"My conscience is clear," said Patrick, "...but I am grieved for my very close friend, ... the one to whom I entrusted my soul!... How did it come to him to disgrace me publicly, in the presence of all?"

"I was mightily upset," Patrick admitted. He would have fallen into despair, but "the Lord generously spared me.... He came powerfully to my assistance in that state of being trampled down."

It appears, from the *Confessions,* that Patrick never understood why his friend betrayed him and was never able to resolve the situation on a human level. The only thing he could do, he tells us, was to pray to God "that it shall not be held as a sin against them that I fell truly into disgrace and scandal."

Do not place much confidence in weak and mortal man, helpful and friendly though he may be. Do not grieve too much if he sometimes opposes and contradicts you. Those who are with us today may be against us tomorrow, and vice versa, for men change with the wind. Place all your trust in God.... He will answer for you; he will do what is best for you.

Thomas à Kempis
The Imitation of Christ

Place no reliance on the opinions and support of [other people]. Today they are on your side; tomorrow they are your enemy. Moreover, observe that when you are in trouble, almost everyone contrives to add to it in some way or other, were it only by doubting your prudence.

St. Mary Euphrasia Pelletier
St. Mary Euphrasia Pelletier: Foundress of the Good Shepherd Sisters

> Don't be offended by people who injure you but rather, in humble patience, mourn for their sins. Have compassion on them and pray fervently for them. To the extent that we suffer and endure injuries and trials patiently for the love of God, so great and no greater are we before him....
>
> It is far more blessed to endure injuries and reproaches patiently, without murmuring, for the love of God than it is to feed a hundred poor men or keep a perpetual fast. What good does it do us—how does it benefit us—to afflict our body with many fasts, vigils, and disciplines if we cannot endure a little injury from a neighbor? And yet from this we might gain greater reward and higher merit than from all self-inflicted penitential sufferings. To endure reproaches and injuries from our neighbor humbly, patiently, without complaint, will purge away our sins faster than if we shed a fountain of tears.
>
> St. Francis of Assisi
> Adapted from *The Little Flowers of St. Francis*

A Heroic Response to a Tragic Marriage

Blessed Victoria Rasoamanarivo could probably have obtained an annulment of her marriage fairly easily. She was only about fourteen when the marriage took place, in 1864 in her native Madagascar. Her non-Christian family had chosen the groom, Radraika, who was not a Catholic. He was a drunkard and, it soon became clear, a profligate adulterer. Radraika was the son of the queen's husband, and Victoria was an attendant of the queen. Nevertheless, once Victoria's domestic plight became evident, both the queen and Radraika's father urged her to divorce Radraika.

Victoria, a devout convert, was convinced that the divorce of someone of her prominent social standing would reflect badly on the Catholic faith in that predominately pagan nation. She had been exceptionally pious before her marriage, and she now channeled her energies into caring for the needy, assisting missionaries, living simply in spite of her wealth—and praying for and quietly influencing Radraika.

She kept up this apostolate for over twenty years, until one day Radraika came home drunk and collapsed. The doctor could do nothing for him. Victoria kept watch beside him for several days, and when he responded positively to her suggestion that he repent of his sins, she summoned a priest. The priest was delayed, and Victoria herself baptized Radraika before he died.

Victoria didn't have to stick with her husband, and her decision to do so might not appeal to many people today. But she felt that the greater good lay in attending to his spiritual need, not her own comfort. On the other hand, she didn't focus all her attention on him and retreat into self-pity. Instead, she worked so zealously on behalf of the Catholic Church in Madagascar that she was largely responsible for its survival during a period of intense persecution. She was "perfect in charity," a Protestant who knew her said. She was "the servant of others," a Catholic added. "It was for this above all that [we] had so much veneration for her."

A Misunderstanding Between Holy Men

The break between St. Basil and St. Gregory Nazianzen was not really a matter of betrayal, but Gregory experienced it as such. Perhaps more than anything, their story illustrates the importance, for quarreling friends, of laying aside hard feelings and reaching genuine reconciliation before it's too late.

Basil and Gregory became friends as students in Athens during the fourth century. They were "a famous pair," Gregory said, "known and boasted of as such among our teachers." Both were devoted to the faith, both were brilliant students, both excelled in philosophy and rhetoric. At the time, neither would have suspected that much later, after nearly twenty-five years of devoted friendship, they would experience a rupture in their relationship that would never quite heal.

After their student days, the two settled down together as hermits. Several years later Basil left to help his bishop in his ongoing battle against heresy, but the friends stayed in touch. Both were ordained, and Basil eventually became bishop of Caesarea. It was in his role as bishop that Basil, in a dispute with the hostile emperor, played his hand too freely (or so Gregory thought).

The situation was complicated, but it boiled down to this: In order to thwart the unfriendly maneuvering of the government, Basil thought he should strengthen his authority over a particular part of his diocese. He did so by appointing Gregory as bishop to Sasima, the disputed territory. Unfortunately, Sasima was a miserable outpost, nothing but dust and dirt, with few houses and a jail so close by that you could hear, Gregory said, the groans of the prisoners and the rattling of their chains. Very reluctantly, he agreed to be consecrated, but he could never bring himself to actually live in the place.

Basil accused Gregory of dereliction of duty. Gregory suspected Basil of self-interest and political motivation and felt betrayed by his old friend. "Well, play the man," he wrote to Basil, "be strong, turn everything to your own glory, as rivers suck up the mountain torrent.... So much shall I gain from this your friendship, not to trust in friends, or to put anything above God."

The damage was done, and while the two later patched up their differences, the friendship was never the same. Gregory remained deeply hurt, and Basil later said of this and his many struggles as bishop, "For my sins I seem to fail at everything."

Gregory outlived Basil by ten years. He came to believe that Basil genuinely had the good of the church at heart in the Sasima incident. Three years after Basil's death, Gregory delivered a moving tribute to him, made all the more poignant by the fact that, humanly speaking, it came too late.

"His thoughts were above the thoughts of men," he said. "Detached from this world while still in it, he referred all things to the Holy Spirit. He knew how to respect friendship and only disdained it when he knew he must put God's honor before everything else. He put the hopes of eternity above human things."

False Confidants

Advanced age is no guarantee against betrayal. Alphonsus Liguori, founder of the Redemptorist Order, was eighty-five, crippled, deaf, almost blind, and weighed down by the administrative duties of his order when he was betrayed by some of his closest friends and advisors, including his confessor.

Liguori and his priests worked in and around the kingdom of Naples in the eighteenth century. The hostile political climate there led to a twenty-four-year vendetta against them in which opponents attempted to suppress the order. A change in political power brought relief, and Liguori, judging the moment favorable, seized the opportunity to have his rule for the congregation approved by the government. Approval would protect them from those who claimed the order was an illegal religious society.

Some of Liguori's own men, who apparently wanted peace at any cost, connived with a priest in the king's service to alter the rule, making it more acceptable to their opponents. They even abolished the religious vows central to Redemptorist identity. The conspirators let the opening words of the document stand but amended the rest in small, cramped lettering with many erasures, making it nearly illegible. Liguori, with his failing eyesight, read only the familiar opening lines and then signed. The king approved, and the rule became legally binding before Liguori realized he had been duped.

"You have founded the congregation and you have destroyed it!" one of his priests told him. Liguori, in anguish, confronted his confessor: "I never thought I could be so deceived by you." The hoax was made more galling by the fact that Liguori, before becoming a priest, had been a brilliant lawyer, said never to have lost a case in his eight years of practice. "It was my duty to read [the rule] myself," he said, "but you know I find it difficult to read even a few lines."

The order remained a shambles for the final six years of Liguori's life, and he didn't have an easy time reconciling himself to the situation. In fact, he endured eighteen months of severe temptations against the faith, as well as inclinations to despair and fear. These struggles eventually resolved, to be followed by interior peace and even ecstasies, prophecies, and miracles. Six years after his death, his order was reconstituted and began to spread around the world, as Liguori had prophesied.

Love Your Enemies

Those on the receiving end of wrongdoing—whether the betrayal of a friend or the malice of an enemy—know how difficult it is to forgive. In this passage, directed to those preparing for baptism in the early church, St. Augustine takes a look at the command in the Lord's Prayer to "forgive those who trespass against us." Failure to forgive leads to anger and resentment and compounds the victim's suffering.

> If anyone sins against you ... forgive him at once. Forgive in your heart, where God sees. People sometimes forgive with their lips ... but cherish resentment in their hearts because they have no respect for God.
>
> I implore you not to be so unkind to your own soul. The cruelest enemy in the world cannot do you as much harm as you do yourself by refusing to forgive him. He can injure your property or your family or your bodily health, but he cannot do the harm to your soul that you yourself can do.
>
> My friends, I urge you to reach out and lay hold of this perfect gift of love, the love of enemies. Do not say to

yourselves, "It is impossible...." If you tell yourself it is impossible, then you will not be able to do it. The first step is to believe it is possible, and then pray that God's will may be done in you....

If we do not forgive we must not count on receiving forgiveness ourselves. Understand this clearly. Anger is a normal human passion, and there is no need to be ashamed of angry feelings, so long as we keep them within bounds. You can be angry, the psalm says, but do not sin (Ps 4:5); that is, do not hold on to the anger in your heart, for if you do it will turn into hatred, which is a deadly sin. Anger is a mere shoot, while hatred is a great tree. Nevertheless, a shoot can grow into a tree if it is not rooted out straight away. By harboring evil suspicions and rash judgments we water that shoot, that first movement of anger and resentment, until it grows into a fully developed tree.

So although angry feelings are natural and not in themselves sinful, they must be dealt with immediately and not allowed to grow into the desire for revenge. Who are we to seek to be avenged? If God chose to be avenged on us, what would become of us? When your enemy comes to you and asks your pardon, forgive him at once. Is this so very difficult? I know it is hard to love someone when he is actually attacking you, but is it so hard to love him when he asks for forgiveness? Yet my ambition for you is even greater than this, for I would hope that even when you are suffering wrong you would turn to the Lord Jesus, recalling his own prayer for his enemies: "Father, forgive them; they do not know what they are doing" (Lk 23:34).

Perhaps you may protest that after all, Jesus was the

Lord, the Son of God, the Word Incarnate—what can be expected of a mere human being? Very well, think of your fellow servant Stephen, who was stoned to death by his enemies. When they forced him to the ground he prayed: "Lord, do not hold this sin against them" (Acts 7:60).

Notice that Stephen's enemies were not asking his forgiveness. They were hurling stones at him. Yet he prayed for them. This is the kind of Christian I want you to be.... Reach out for this perfect gift which is the love of one's enemies. Why go dragging your heart in the dust? Lift it up to the Lord; believe in the power he has given you to overcome yourself. Love those who hate you, then all the world will know that you are children of your Father in heaven.

St. Augustine
From Darkness to Light

There are in fact two kinds of martyrdom. One takes place only in the heart, the other in both heart and body. We too are capable of being martyrs, even without having anyone slay us. To die from someone's enmity is martyrdom out in the open; to bear insults, to love a person who hates us, is martyrdom in secret.

St. Gregory the Great
Be Friends of God

THREE

THE WEIGHT OF THE CROSS: SICKNESS AND DEATH

It's not often that a saint names one type of suffering as more difficult than any other. St. John Chrysostom, bishop of Constantinople in the fourth century, did so. He himself had suffered everything from the death of loved ones to betrayal to illness. Eventually he ended up in exile and died there, a victim of government efforts to interfere in the life of the church. This he found so lonely and oppressive that he spoke of it as "indescribable solitude, daily death." But in a letter from exile to his good friend Olympias, he zeroed in on physical suffering as most debilitating of all.

Olympias was frequently seriously ill herself, and it is possible that Chrysostom's enthusiasm for his topic is colored by his efforts to encourage her. But he tells her that nothing—not exile, imprisonment, abuse, not even death, "terrible and loathsome as it may be—is so oppressive as infirmity of the body." He backs up his claim with the biblical story of Job, who managed to endure the loss of everything until "he was delivered up to sickness and sores." Then he began "to long for death ... [and] bewail and lament, so that you may understand that this type of suffering is more severe than all others, and this form of patience [in the face of pain] the highest of all."

Regardless of which type of suffering is the most difficult, many saints speak to the extraordinary pain inflicted both by illness and death. St. Basil wept inconsolably on hearing of the death of a friend's son. In such circumstances, "who is so stony-hearted or so entirely devoid of human sympathy ... as to give his soul to only moderate grief?" he wrote to the father. "A lifetime will not suffice ... to deplore this misfortune," he said, aligning himself forever with anyone coping with similar anguish.

The saints treat the sick, the dying, and the grieving with great compassion. They do not mean for their reflections to be intrusive; they tend to offer them out of a sense of solidarity. The saints don't completely answer the questions most on the minds of the sick and grieving—Why this? Why me?—but they stand alongside the suffering in their need, helping them lean into God for solace and strength.

Bearing Illness

Sickness is a far better proof of what we really are than health, and the bravest of us are tempted by impatience and depression under the test of pain....
O Savior, you yourself suffered so much. You died to win our salvation and also to show how God may be glorified in the bearing of pain. Teach us to realize the great treasure that lies hidden in the state of sickness.

St. Vincent de Paul
Some Counsels of St. Vincent de Paul

Illness and suffering have always been among the gravest problems confronted in human life. In illness, man experiences his powerlessness, his limitations, and his finitude. Every illness can make us glimpse death.

Illness can lead to anguish, self-absorption, sometimes even despair and revolt against God. It can also make a person more mature, helping him discern in his life what is not essential so he can turn toward that which is. Very often, illness provokes a search for God and a return to him....

Christ's compassion toward the sick and his many healings of every kind of infirmity are a resplendent sign that "God has visited his people" and that the Kingdom of God is close at hand. Jesus has the power not only to heal but also to forgive sins; he has come to heal the whole man, soul and body; he is the physician the sick have need of....

But [Christ] did not heal all the sick. His healings ... announced a more radical healing: the victory over sin and death through his Passover. On the cross, Christ took upon himself the whole weight of evil and took away "the sin of the world," of which illness is only a consequence. By his passion and death on the cross Christ has given a new meaning to suffering; it can henceforth configure us to him and unite us with his redemptive passion.

Catechism of the Catholic Church

St. John Eudes wrote the following to a friend who was seriously ill. He advises her to resign herself to her illness because she will find Christ there, supporting, loving, and perfecting her.

[Jesus] is there; ... he abides within you. He is present in your anguish and sufferings. He is there, all love and completely transformed into love for your sake. He is there preparing and ordaining these sufferings through love of you.

He is there, guiding and leading you along the paths of

his love, drawing you toward the perfection of love by means of these trials and severities.

He is there, bearing with you through his love all the anguish of mind and body that is yours to bear. Even though you may often be unaware of it, he is nevertheless infallibly present....

He is there for the purpose of filling you completely with love for him, and much more so than you are filled with suffering.... Not only does he wish to imbue you with his love, but also to transform you entirely into love for him through crosses and sufferings, as his cross and sufferings transformed him into love for us...

May Christ crucified be ever blessed for giving you a share in the sufferings of his cross!

...I see an infinite number of crucified persons in the world, but few who are crucified by the love of Jesus. Some are crucified by their self-love and inordinate love of the world, but happy are they who are crucified for the love of Jesus; happy are they who live and die on the cross with Jesus. You will be numbered among these ... if you bear your cross lovingly, like Jesus.

St. John Eudes
Letters and Shorter Works

St. Jane Frances de Chantal felt that sickness itself can be a form of prayer.

In time ... of bodily sickness, when the heart is often much weakened and without power of prayer, we must not oblige ourselves to try to pray, because simple acts of consent to the will of God, from time to time, are quite enough. In any case, suffering which is borne by the will, with patience and gentleness, forms an unending and all-powerful prayer in the sight of God, in spite of the complaining and anxiety which may be felt in our lower nature.

St. Jane Frances de Chantal
The Jewels of St. Jane Frances de Chantal

A Saintly Man Confronts Epilepsy

Venerable Francis Libermann's struggle with epilepsy threatened to derail his plans to become a priest and plunged him, from time to time, into deep depression. Libermann, a seminarian in France, was about twenty-six years old in 1828, when the seizures began. Previously he had experienced severe headaches and waves of weakness but now, when he was worn out by his studies, the headaches became disabling. He compared them to a steel band clamped around his head.

One day Libermann went to the infirmary to visit a fellow seminarian who was sick. As he sat down, he experienced his first full-blown seizure, falling to the floor as convulsions ripped through his rigid body. His head beat against the floor, and bloody foam seeped from his mouth. When the tremors stopped, Libermann slipped into a deep, protracted sleep.

A few weeks later, climbing the stairs with a heavy load of books, Libermann sensed an impending attack and, to avoid falling down the stairs, threw himself forward into a hallway as he was again gripped by a severe seizure. From then on the attacks came frequently, almost always preceded by a warning sense followed by serious convulsions, bone-deep fatigue, and growing temptations to despair.

Men with seizure disorders were barred from the priesthood, and Libermann was no exception. In 1831, three years after the illness began, Libermann had to abandon his studies. His superiors thought very highly of the intelligent, compassionate young man, however, and asked him to stay on and help out at their house for incoming seminarians.

Libermann's epilepsy persisted. He often spoke with slurred, halting speech and once told a friend that he felt as if something were tearing his insides apart and that he experienced "frightful" pain. Further, his suffering and sense of discouragement led to depression and temptations to suicide. He often went into Paris on errands, and each time he crossed a bridge over the Seine, he later recalled, he had to fight the urge to throw himself into the river below.

Libermann used the humiliations and suffering of his illness as an opportunity to gain control of his sensitive, quick-tempered personality and to forge an interior sense of peace and abandonment to God's will. Eventually the seizures ended, and although he continued to have what he called "nervous spells"—periods of tension and headache—and still had difficulty with his speech, he was ordained in 1841. Not long after, he founded a missionary order, which he later merged with the Congregation of the Holy Ghost. He is considered the second founder of the Holy Ghost Fathers.

Libermann's suffering helped him develop a profound appreciation for the suffering and needs of others. He had keen insight into the human personality and became a sensitive and enormously successful spiritual director. He mentally traded places with people he had to deal with, a friend said, and imagined how he would feel if someone treated him as he was about to treat them. Based perhaps on his own experience, he viewed difficulties as important to the formation and maturation of character and concluded in the long run that all "we have to do is be faithful in following God's guidance and give him a free hand with us."

The Pain of Grief

In about A.D. 358 St. Basil, Bishop of Caesarea, wrote the following letter to a mother on the death of her son. The "crushing misfortune," he said, drove him to "many tears."

> I know how deep are the affections of mothers, and when I ponder the kindliness and gentleness which you in particular show toward all, I realize how great must be your grief in the present circumstance. You have lost a son whom, while he lived, all mothers blessed and prayed that their own sons might resemble and, when he died, all bewailed as if each one had buried her own.... O earth, forced to endure such a calamity! Well might the sun, had it possessed a sense of feeling, have shuddered at that sad spectacle.
>
> However, God's providence orders all circumstances of our life, for we have learned from the Gospel that not even a sparrow falls without the will of the Father.... Let us accept what has befallen us; for we do not improve our lot by bearing it unwillingly but rather, destroy ourselves.... The Lord is making a trial of your love for him. Yours is the opportunity of receiving through patient endurance the portion allotted to martyrs.... Great is the suffering, I do admit, but great also are the rewards reserved by the Lord for those who endure....

The untimeliness of [your son's] death grieves us. Yet, that this is not a timely death is not certain, since we ourselves do not know how to choose most advantageously for our souls nor how to determine the limits appointed for the life of men....

Do not measure your suffering in itself alone, for in this way it will appear unbearable to you, but compare it with all human happenings, and therein you will find consolation. Above all I have this to say most forcefully: "Have consideration for your husband; be a comfort one to the other; do not make the affliction harder for him to bear by wearing yourself out with grief."

On the whole, I do not think that words alone suffice for consolation, but I believe that there is need of prayer under the present circumstances. Therefore, I pray the Lord himself, by touching your heart with his ineffable power, [will] enlighten your soul through the good use of reason, so that you may have from within yourself the sources of consolation.

St. Basil
Fathers of the Church

[Paul said], "We do not want you to be unaware, brothers, about those who have fallen asleep, so that you may not grieve like the rest, who have no hope" [1 Thess 4:13]. He did not say "about the dying" but "about those who have fallen asleep," proving that death is a sleep. When we see someone sleeping we are not disturbed or distressed, expecting that he will certainly get up. Even so, when we see anyone dead, let us not be disturbed or dejected, for this also is a sleep, a longer one indeed, but still a sleep.

By giving it the name of slumber, Paul comforted the mourners and overthrew the accusation of the unbelievers. If you mourn immoderately over someone who has departed, you will be like that unbeliever who has no hope of a resurrection.... But you have received such strong proofs concerning the future life, why do you sink into the same weakness with him? Therefore it is written: "We do not want you to be unaware, brothers, about those who have fallen asleep, so that you may not grieve like the rest who have no hope."

St. John Chrysostom
Adapted from *The Nicene and Post Nicene Fathers*

The Death of a Holy Mother

Blessed Frederick Ozanam, founder of the St. Vincent de Paul Society, credited his mother with instilling in him a love for the poor. "Happy the man to whom God gives a holy mother!" he wrote. His account of her death, in the presence of Ozanam and his brothers, describes the paradox felt by many Christians in similar circumstances: desolation mixed with peace and the hope of reunion.

There were no convulsions, no agony, only a slumber that left her countenance almost smiling, a faint breathing that grew gradually fainter, until at last it ceased and we rose up orphans. How shall I describe the desolation that broke forth then, and at the same time the inexpressible, incomprehensible inward peace that we all felt, the sense of a new blessedness that, in spite of ourselves, filled our hearts to overflowing...

Often in our solitude now, in the midst of the anguish that weighs down my soul, the remembrance of that august scene returns to sustain and uplift me. I think of how short life is, how soon we shall be reunited with those from whom death has parted us, and then I feel all temptations of self-love, all the unworthy instincts of my nature, fade away and my desires are concentrated in the single one of dying like my mother.

Blessed Frederic Ozanam
Frederic Ozanam: His Life and Works

Two years after his mother died, Ozanam wrote to console a friend who had just lost his mother. He expanded on the sense of peace and "new blessedness" that he mentioned in the preceding excerpt.

Nothing is so appalling as the growing solitude, the void that death creates around us. I have gone through it all but this state did not last long. There followed quickly another, when I began to *feel* that I was not alone, when I was conscious of something infinitely sweet in the depths of my soul. It was like an assurance that I had not been left alone; it was a benign though invisible neighborhood; it was as if a cherished soul, passing close by, touched me with its wings. And just as formerly I used to recognize the step, the voice, the breath of my mother, so now when a fresh breeze revived my strength, when a virtuous thought entered my mind, when a salutary impulse stirred my will,

I could not but think it was still my mother.

After a lapse of two years, when time might have dispelled what was merely the effect of an overwrought imagination, I still experience the same thing. There are moments when a sudden thrill passes through me, as if she were there by my side.... Then I shed more abundant tears, perhaps, than in the first months of my bereavement, but an ineffable peace is mingled with their sadness.

When I am good, when I have done anything for the poor, whom she loved so tenderly, when I am at peace with God, whom she served so well, I see her smiling on me in the distance. Sometimes, when I am praying, I fancy I hear her voice praying with me, as we used to do together at the foot of the crucifix every night. Often, in fact—this I would not breathe to anyone, but I confide it to you—when I have the happiness [to receive Communion], when our Savior comes to visit me, it is as if she followed him into my wretched heart, as many a time she followed him when he was born in Viaticum to the dwellings of the poor. *And then I believe firmly in the real presence of my mother near me.*

Blessed Frederic Ozanam
Frederic Ozanam: His Life and Works

Martyrdom: A Fact of Christian Life

We must all stand prepared for the battle.... The Lord desired that we should rejoice and leap for joy in persecutions because, when persecutions occur, then are given the crowns of faith, then the soldiers of God are proved, then the heavens are opened to martyrs. For we have not in such a way given our name to warfare that we ought only to think about peace, and draw back and refuse war. When in this very warfare, the Lord walked first—the teacher of humility, and endurance, and suffering—so that what he taught to be done, he first of all did, and what he exhorts to suffer, he himself first suffered for us.

St. Cyprian
Days of the Lord III

And if anyone believes not that death is abolished, that Hell is trodden underfoot, that the chains thereof are broken, that the tyrant is bound, let him look on the martyrs deporting themselves in the presence of death, and taking up the jubilant strain of the victory of Christ. O the marvel! Since the hour when Christ despoiled hell, men have danced in triumph over death. "O death, where is thy sting? O grave, where is thy victory?"

St. Gregory Thaumaturgus
Ante-Nicene Fathers

Martyrdom—dying for the faith—is possible in any age, as is evident in the bloody witness given by many Christians during the twentieth century. Joseph Kowalski, a young Salesian priest, was one of these modern martyrs, dying at the hands of the Nazis during World War II.

A native of Poland, Kowalski had been ordained only three years when his zealous pastoral work, especially among young people, attracted the attention of the occupying German forces. The Nazis arrested him and sent him to Auschwitz concentration camp. There they subjected him to particularly brutal treatment out of hatred for the priesthood.

Nevertheless, he kept up a lively (though forbidden) pastoral ministry behind the barbed wire. "He gave absolution to the dying," a fellow inmate testified, "he strengthened those who were discouraged, uplifted spiritually the poor souls awaiting the death sentence, brought them Communion secretly, and even managed to organize holy Mass in the huts, as well as leading prayers and helping the needy."

Kowalski was devoted to Mary and often prayed the rosary, which he kept with him at all times. On one occasion he was part of a line-up of prisoners to be transported to Dachau. An officer noticed that the priest clutched something in one hand. "What are you holding?" the Nazi asked. When Kowalski remained silent, the officer hit his hand, knocking the rosary to the ground. He ordered the priest to trample it. When Kowalski refused, the officer pulled him out of the transport. "We understood," a fellow inmate said, "that because of the rosary, severe punishment lay ahead of him."

Eventually it became clear that the Nazis had targeted Kowalski for death. "It was early in July 1942 and the day was very hot," a witness said. "The guards were going mad in their mania for killing people, and they were amusing themselves with acts of cruelty." They drowned some prisoners in a cesspool and threw others into the muddy waters of a canal. The guards took those who survived this treatment to a huge empty barrel which was lying on its side and served as a refuge for the camp dogs. "There they were compelled to imitate the dogs by barking," the witness said, "and then lick up from the ground soup that had been thrown down there to feed them."

"Finally, the head guard shouted, 'Where is that Catholic priest? Let him bless them for their journey into eternity.' Meanwhile," the witness continued, "other torturers were throwing Fr. Kowalski (it was he they were looking for) into the mud for their entertainment. Now ... they dragged him to the barrel. Pulled out naked from the cesspool with only tattered trousers clinging to him, dripping from head to foot in that horrible sticky mess of mud and filth and driven forward by furious beatings, he came to the barrel.... The thugs ... made him get up on the barrel and give to the dying 'the final blessing for their journey to paradise, according to the Catholic rite.'"

Fr. Kowalski knelt and made the sign of the cross, proclaiming it in a loud voice. Then he slowly and forcefully recited the Our Father, the Hail Mary, the Salve Regina.

"The words of eternal truth contained in the divine phrases of the Lord's Prayer made a vivid impression on the prisoners," said the inmate, who with several others watched the scene from a hiding place. "We tasted the words of Fr. Kowalski as material food for the peace we longed for.... We witnessed the sublime mystery celebrated by Fr. Kowalski against that macabre backdrop. [A companion] whispered in my ear: 'A prayer like that the world has never heard.... Perhaps they did not pray like that even in the catacombs.'"

Later that night the Nazis drowned Kowalski in the camp cesspool. Pope John Paul II beatified the priest—now known as Blessed Joseph Kowalski—in 1999.

FOUR

TRIALS OF THE SPIRIT: TEMPTATION AND DOUBT

Temptations come in many forms, but it was the temptations of sex that nearly defeated St. Augustine. Augustine was a professor of rhetoric and grammar in the late third and early fourth centuries. Raised a Catholic, he abandoned the faith when he went away to school. He took a mistress when he was eighteen, and together they had a son.

Throughout early adulthood Augustine searched for truth, joining the Manichean sect before gradually drawing near again to Christianity. He broke up with his mistress, but "the fetters of lust" held him, he said. "Give me chastity ... but not yet," he had prayed as an adolescent, and now that he was an adult he was reaping the consequences: "Sin became a habit, and habit, once indulged, became a necessity." The struggle "tore my soul apart," he said, and in an effort to dodge this and other issues, "I hid behind my own back, refusing to see myself." Augustine knew he could marry, but even at this point felt attracted to—and yet was clearly repelled by—the celibate life.

In the eighth book of his autobiographical *Confessions* Augustine described his conflict in detail, culminating with his dramatic conversion. He suffered heroically but succeeded in the end.

Augustine's battle is a very contemporary one, as are the struggles of other saints with various temptations, especially against the faith. The lives of St. Thérèse of Lisieux and St. Jane Frances de Chantal are particularly interesting in that these women struggled with their doubts when they were well into mature faith: St. Jane de Chantal, for most of her adult life; St. Thérèse, suddenly, after a lifetime of untroubled belief.

In whatever form temptation comes, the saints see it as an inescapable fact of life. They face the issue squarely and encourage their readers to do the same.

Confronting Temptation

St. Francis de Sales gives St. Jane de Chantal advice on making a spirited defense against temptation.

> Temptations against the faith go straight to the understanding, to make it parley and dream and think about them. Do you know what you must do when the enemy is occupied trying to scale the intellect? Sally out by the gate of the will and make a good attack against him.
>
> That is, when a temptation against the faith comes to engage you ("How can this be?" "But what if this...?" "But what if that...?") instead of disputing with the enemy by argument, let your affective part rush forth vehemently upon him ... cry ... 'Get thee behind me, Satan!'...
>
> You must also say words to Jesus Christ and to the Holy Spirit (such as he will suggest to you) and even to the church ....
>
> Fight back with affections and not with reasons, with passions of the heart and not with considerations of the mind. It is true that in these times of temptation the poor will is quite dry, but so much the better. Its acts will be so much the more terrible to the enemy, who, seeing that instead of

retarding your progress he gives you an opportunity of exercising a thousand virtuous affections, and particularly the protestation of faith, will leave you at last.

St. Francis de Sales
St. Francis de Sales: Selected Letters

Fear and anxiety can be deeply troubling to the spirit. Those prone to anxiety as well as those dealing with frightening circumstances will benefit from this meditation of St. Francis de Sales.

St. Peter, says the Scripture, seeing the storm, which was very fierce, was afraid; and as soon as he became afraid, he began to sink and drown, at which he cried, "O Lord, save me." And our Lord took him by the hand, and said to him, "Man of little faith, why didst thou doubt?" Regard this holy apostle. He walks dry-footed on the waters; the waves and the wind could not make him sink, but the fear of the wind and the waves makes him perish if his Master does not rescue him.

Fear is a greater evil than the evil itself.... Fear not; you walk on the sea, amid the winds and the waves, but it is with Jesus. What is there to fear? But if fear seizes you, cry loudly, "O Lord, save me." He will give you his hand; clasp it tight, go joyously on. To sum up, do not philosophize about your trouble, do not turn in upon yourself; go straight on. No, God cannot lose you, so long as you live in your resolution not to lose him. Let the world turn upside down, let everything be in darkness, in smoke, in uproar—God is with us.

St. Francis de Sales
Thy Will Be Done

Struggles of the Little Flower

During her final year of life St. Thérèse of Lisieux suffered extreme pain from the tuberculosis that would eventually kill her. Worse than the physical pain, however, was her daily struggle for faith. In contrast to her previous and lifelong experience of God, she was now tempted to despair, unbelief, and the fear that God didn't love her and that heaven didn't exist. She rarely felt any relief from these doubts but held on through sheer determination, forcing herself to believe with her mind what she no longer felt in her spirit. She actually welcomed the fight, offering her sufferings up for the needs of others.

In her autobiography, *The Story of a Soul*, St. Thérèse discusses these temptations against faith:

> Jesus ... allowed pitch-black darkness to sweep over my soul and let the thought of heaven, so sweet to me from my infancy, destroy all my peace and torture me. This trial was not something lasting a few days or weeks. I suffered it for months and am still waiting for it to end.
>
> I wish I could express what I feel but it is impossible. One must have travelled through the same sunless tunnel to understand how dark it is....
>
> My sufferings increased whenever I grew wearied by the surrounding darkness and tried to find peace and strength by thinking of eternal life. For the voice of unbelievers came to mock me out of the darkness: "You dream of light, of a fragrant land, you dream that their Creator will be yours forever, and you think you will one day leave behind

this fog in which you languish. Hope on! Hope on! And look forward to death! But it will give you, not what you hope for, but a still darker night, the night of annihilation!"

...This story of my suffering is as inadequate as an artist's sketch compared with his model, but I do not want to write any more about it lest I should blaspheme. I am afraid I have already said too much.

May God forgive me! He knows very well that although I had not the consolation of faith, I forced myself to act as if I had. I have made more acts of faith in the last year than in the whole of my life.

St. Thérèse of Lisieux
The Story of a Soul

In the following Thérèse addresses herself to the superior of her convent, describing the determination with which she met the challenge.

My dear Mother, I may perhaps appear to you to be exaggerating my trial. In fact, if you are judging according to the sentiments I express in my little poems composed this year, I must appear to you as a soul filled with consolations and one for whom the veil of faith is almost torn aside; and yet, it is no longer a veil for me, it is a wall which reaches right up to the heavens and covers the starry firmament. When I sing of the happiness of heaven and of the eternal possession of God, I feel no joy in this, for I sing simply what *I want to believe.* It is true that at times a very small ray of the sun comes to illumine my darkness,

> and then the trial ceases for an instant, but afterwards the memory of this ray, instead of causing me joy, makes my darkness even more dense.
>
> St. Thérèse of Lisieux
> *The Story of a Soul*

St. Thérèse's temptations against the faith troubled her chaplain, but Thérèse herself saw them as a sort of martyrdom of spirit that would not only test her but also benefit others. On the one hand, she offered them up as a sacrifice for sinners; on the other hand, she could serve as a model of hope and patient endurance for others similarly tested by doubt.

> Ah! I'm not pretending, it's very true that I don't see a thing. But I must sing very strongly in my heart: "After death life is immortal," or without this, things would turn out badly.
>
> It is upon heaven that everything hinges. How strange and incoherent this is.
>
> Must one love God and the Blessed Virgin so much and still have thoughts like this? But I don't dwell on them.
>
> What darkness! However, I am still at peace!
>
> St. Thérèse of Lisieux
> *The Story of a Soul*

No One Escapes Temptation

The Imitation of Christ offers practical advice for combating temptation: Dig it up at its root; don't entertain it; never despair.

As long as we live in this world we cannot escape suffering and temptation: "The life of humanity on earth is a warfare," we read in Job. Therefore, we must all guard against temptation and watch in prayer so that the devil, who never sleeps but goes about seeking people to devour, is unable to deceive us. Not one of us is so perfect or holy that we are above being tempted. We can never be completely free from temptation.

Yet temptations, though troublesome and severe, are often useful to us for they humble, purify, and instruct us. The saints all passed through many temptations and trials and profited by them.... There is no state so holy, no place so secret, that temptations and trials will not come. We are never safe from them as long as we live because they come from within us—in sin we were born. When one temptation or trial passes, another comes. We shall always have something to suffer because we have lost the state of original blessedness.

Many people try to escape temptations only to fall more deeply. We cannot conquer simply by fleeing. Instead, we need patience and true humility to become stronger than all our enemies. If we only shun temptations outwardly but fail to uproot them, we won't make much progress. Indeed, the temptations will return more violently than before.

Little by little, in patience and long-suffering, by the

help of God rather than severity,... we will overcome them. We should frequently take counsel when tempted. And just as we ourselves want to be consoled when we are tempted, so we should console others when they are tempted, avoiding all harshness toward them....

Above all, we must be especially alert against the beginnings of temptation, for we conquer the enemy more easily if we refuse to let him into our mind, if we meet him beyond the threshold when he knocks....

Some suffer great temptations at the beginning of their conversion, others toward the end of life, while some are troubled almost constantly throughout their life. Others are tested but only lightly....

We should not despair, therefore, when we are tempted, but pray fervently to God to help us. According to St. Paul, he will never let us be tempted beyond our strength. Let us humble ourselves under the hand of God in every trial and temptation for he will save and exalt the humble in spirit.

Thomas à Kempis
The Imitation of Christ

On the Calm Defeat of Temptation

Now there is no one who approaches God with a clean and upright heart who is not tested by hardships and temptations. So in all these temptations, see to it that even if you feel them, you do not consent to them but bear them patiently and calmly with humility and long-suffering. Even if they are blasphemies and sordid, hold firmly to this fact in everything, that you can do nothing better or more effective against them than to consider all this sort of fantasy as a nothing. Even if they are the most vile, sordid, horrible blasphemies, simply take no notice of them, count them as nothing, and despise them.

Don't look on them as yours or allow yourself to make them a matter of conscience. The enemy will certainly take flight if you treat him and his company with contempt in this way. He is very proud and cannot bear to be despised and spurned. So the best remedy is to completely ignore these temptations....

The servant of Jesus Christ must see to it that he is not so easily forced to withdraw from the face of the Lord and to be annoyed, murmur, and complain over a ... temptation, suspicion, sadness, ... or any such adversity, when they can all be put to flight with no more than the hand of a good will directed up to God. After all, through a good will [the intention to please God], a man has God as his defender, and the holy angels as his guardians and protectors. What is more, any temptation can be overcome by a good will, too, like a fly driven away from a bald head by one's hand.

To be tempted is not a sin but the opportunity to exercise virtue. Temptation can be greatly to man's benefit, since it is held that "the whole of man's life on earth is a testing (Job 7:1)."

Attributed to St. Albert the Great
On Cleaving to God

There is consolation for those who experience prayer as an occasion of suffering.

> Should [prayer] be accompanied by violent temptations, dryness, and afflictions, which might make me more humble, *that* I should consider to be an excellent kind of prayer....
>
> Let us not imagine that he who suffers does not pray: rather does he the more offer his troubles to God. Often such a one prays better than those who, all alone in their cell, strike their breasts again and again, and when they force themselves to shed a few tears, call that prayer.
>
> St. Teresa of Avila
> *The Letters of Saint Teresa*

Glorious Victory

Blessed Giles of Assisi, an early follower of St. Francis of Assisi, appears often in the book *The Little Flowers of St. Francis.* In this excerpt he explains to his fellow monks the seemingly contradictory nature of suffering and the great good to be gained from overcoming temptations.

> [Brother Giles said that] the more acceptable people are to God, the more furiously the evil one attacks them. Therefore, according to the grace God gives them, they must keep up unceasing warfare. The fiercer the conflict, the more glorious the victor's crown.
>
> The truth is, though, that people who walk carefully in the way of God won't feel fatigue on the journey. People

who walk on the broad way of the world, however, will never be free of labor, weariness, anguish, tribulation, and pain, right up to the day of death.

One of the brothers then said to Brother Giles: "It seems to me that you're teaching us two conflicting things. First, the more virtuous and acceptable to God people are, the greater the conflicts they must endure in the spiritual life. But then you say the opposite—that those who walk carefully in the way of God won't feel weariness or fatigue on the journey."

"It is most certain," Brother Giles answered, "that the devils bring more fearful temptations against those who have a good will than against those who have not. But what harm can the devils and all evil do to those who move ahead discreetly and fervently in the way of God, and work faithfully, aware that their reward will be a thousand times greater than their labor? Truly, those on fire with the fire of divine love, the more fiercely tempted to sin they are, the more deeply will they detest it.

"The worst of the devils rush to tempt those who feel some bodily weakness or infirmity, or who are in great sorrow or anguish, or are tepid, or who are hungry or thirsty, or have been insulted or suffer spiritual or temporal injury. Those wicked spirits know that at those times, in those circumstances, people are most open to temptation.

"But I tell you truly that for every vice and temptation people overcome, they acquire a virtue. For every vice they conquer, they earn a greater grace and a brighter crown."

Bl. Giles of Assisi

Adapted from *The Little Flowers of St. Francis of Assisi*

A Holy Woman's Struggle

St. Jane Frances de Chantal had been happily married for eight years when her husband was killed in a hunting accident. Soon after, she began to experience severe temptations that led her to question everything, from God's care for her to the faith itself. This trial kept up with varying degrees of intensity for the remaining forty-one years of her life: "When I feel cut off like this, even slightly, I think I am teetering on the brink of despair, but I cannot give up ... as long as I am assured that God wants me to endure it."

St. Francis de Sales, her spiritual director and cofounder with her of the Visitation order of nuns, suggested various remedies. "You're too much of a perfectionist about the purity of your faith," he wrote to her. "Let the slightest little doubt creep in, and you think it spoils everything." He advised her to "bend like a reed in the wind," careful not to mistake "the rustling of leaves for the rattling of sabers."

Jane, who revered de Sales, accepted his insights and eventually learned to handle her doubts with a certain degree of confidence. But it never got any easier. "Most often," she wrote late in her life, "there is a confused sort of strife in my soul: between feelings of being plunged into impenetrable darkness, of being powerless to do anything about it myself. I have wandering thoughts, doubts, and a kind of spiritual nausea that tempts me to give up trying, together with all kinds of other miserable feelings. When these trials are at their most severe, they hardly let up at all, and they cause me unimaginable torment.... On the one hand, I am caught between the excruciating pain, and on the other, my love for our holy faith is so deep I would die rather than deny the least article of it.

"I can hardly believe God would permit anyone to go through this, and yet, no matter how long the pain lasts, somehow I find the strength to hold on."

Occasionally Jane experienced brief assurances that God was with her and sustaining her. "After I saw that God was holding me up," she said, "I would feel the tiniest bit of peace and interior security."

In spite of her torments, Jane was a woman of great charm and intelligence, with a charismatic personality and excellent business instincts. Her personal struggles never interfered with her work life. "It is a kind of dilemma that ... does not keep me from doing work, writing, talking about business and other things."

St. Vincent de Paul knew Jane well. "She was full of faith," he said of her, "yet all her life long ... tormented by thoughts against it. While apparently enjoying that peace and easiness of mind of souls who have reached a high state of virtue, she suffered such interior trial that she often told me her mind was so filled with all sorts of temptations and abominations that she had to strive not to look within herself, for she could not bear it.... But for all that suffering, her face never lost its serenity, nor did she once relax in the fidelity God asked of her. And so I regard her as one of the holiest souls I have ever met on this earth."

God's Amazing Grace

The grace to overcome temptation is always available to us, even if we don't want it.

> The Lord has given us our post in the battle against powerful foes; but he is faithful in his promises and will never allow us to be assaulted more violently than we can resist: "God is faithful and will not let you be tried beyond your strength" [1 Cor 10:13]. He is faithful, since he instantly helps the man who invokes him.
>
> The learned Cardinal Gotti writes that God has bound himself not only to give us grace precisely balancing the temptation that assails us, but that he is obliged, when we are tempted and turn to him, to give us, by means of that grace which is kept ready for and offered to all, sufficient strength for us actually to resist the temptation.
>
> "God is bound, when we are tempted and fly to his protection, to give us by the grace prepared and offered to all, such strength as will not only put us in the way of being able to resist, but will also make us resist; 'for we can do all things in him who strengthens us' by his grace, if we humbly ask for it."
>
> We can do all things with God's help, which is granted to everyone who humbly seeks it; so that we have no excuse when we allow ourselves to be overcome by a temptation. We are conquered solely by our own fault, because we would not pray. By prayer all the snares and power of the devil are easily overcome. "By prayer, all hurtful things are chased away," says St. Augustine.

St. Alphonsus Liguori
The Great Means of Salvation and of Perfection

FIVE

FIGHTING BACK: PRAYER AND OTHER HELPS IN TIME OF NEED

Venerable Matt Talbot took his first drink at the age of twelve and then drank steadily for the next sixteen years. He managed to hold a job as a dockworker but spent his pay on liquor, sometimes pawning his shirt and boots for the price of a drink. He occasionally stole to support his habit, once stealing a fiddle from a poor, blind, itinerant musician.

Talbot was twenty-eight when he quit drinking, spurred by an incident with his friends. One day he happened to be broke, but his drinking buddies refused to buy him a pint, even though he always stood for them when they were broke. Their indifference served as a wake-up call, and Talbot "took the pledge" for sobriety. He never touched alcohol for the remaining forty-one years of his life.

Talbot sustained his difficult commitment with all the means the church provides for those coping with personal suffering. He attended daily Mass, received daily Communion, paid frequent visits to the Blessed Sacrament, read lives of the saints and other spiritual books, confided in a spiritual director, developed a profound prayer life, fasted, went to confession frequently, and practiced penance. He was also devoted to Mary and found good companions through a Jesuit lay society that he joined. Actually, he carried his program to the extreme and lived like a monk in the midst of the world.

While his regimen can't be imitated in every respect (it was found, when he died, that he wore chains around his body, under his clothes), his story illustrates the role of the spiritual life in handling suffering. The resources that helped Talbot can help everyone, as the saints, in the following, make clear.

The Power of Prayer

St. Alphonsus Liguori insists on the importance of prayer to those suffering in body or mind.

> What is prayer? It is, St. John Chrysostom says, "the anchor of those tossed on the sea, the treasure of the poor, the cure of diseases, the safeguard of health." It is a secure anchor for him who is in peril of shipwreck; it is a treasury of immense wealth for him who is poor; it is a most efficacious medicine for him who is sick....
>
> What does prayer effect? Let us hear St. Laurence Justinian: "It pleases God, it gets what it asks, it overcomes enemies, it changes men." It appeases the wrath of God, who pardons all who pray with humility. It obtains every grace that is asked for; it vanquishes all the strength of the tempter, and it changes men from blind into seeing, from weak into strong, from sinners into saints.
>
> St. Alphonsus Liguori
> *The Great Means of Salvation and of Perfection*

❁

Prayer can take Christians beyond their pain, into the company of Christ.

> The more we suffer and the more we are tempted, the more we should pray. In prayer is our only help, our only strength, our only consolation. We pray that the pain and power of temptation will not paralyze our prayer. The devil puts forth all his strength to stop it at such times. But far from yielding to this temptation, far from yielding to the natural weakness that would like to see the soul absorbed in its pain and conscious of nothing else, we must look for our Savior who is there, close to us, and we must talk with him. He is before us, looking lovingly upon us, straining to hear us, telling us to speak to him, telling us that he is there, that he loves us.
>
> Venerable Charles de Foucauld
> *Spiritual Autobiography of Charles de Foucauld*

> Prayer is the most necessary weapon of defense against our enemies; he who does not avail himself of it, says St. Thomas, is lost. He does not doubt that the reason of Adam's fall was because he did not recommend himself to God when he was tempted: "He sinned because he had not recourse to the divine assistance." St. Gelasius says the same of the rebel angels: "Receiving the grace of God in vain, they could not persevere because they did not pray." St. Charles Borromeo, in a pastoral letter, observes that among all the means of salvation recommended by Jesus

> Christ in the Gospel, the first place is given to prayer....
>
> In darkness, distress, and danger, we have no other hope than to raise our eyes to God and with fervent prayers to beseech his mercy to save us.
>
> St. Alphonsus Liguori
> *The Great Means of Salvation and of Perfection*

It can be more painful to watch those we love suffer than to suffer ourselves. Elisabeth Leseur suggests steps to help deal with this common situation.

> It is comparatively easy not to be absorbed in our own suffering, but the suffering of those we love is apt to become a constant and unhappy obsession, against which we must struggle: first by prayer, confiding those we love to God in complete filial abandonment, then by work, and also by an occupation chosen outside the center of our thoughts and affections. Finally, by doing good to others, we can try to forget a little of our dear ones' burdens, which are a thousand times more painful than the ones we carry alone.
>
> Elisabeth Leseur
> *My Spirit Rejoices*

Seek the Lord

The Imitation of Christ urges quick action when faced with trials.

I am the Lord who sends comfort in time of tribulation. Come, therefore, to me when it is not well with you. What hinders you most is that you turn yourself to me too slowly; before you pray heartily to me you seek many other comforts and refresh your spirit in outward things. And so it comes about that all you do helps you little, until you can behold and see that I am he who sends comfort to all who faithfully call to me, and that without me there can be no profitable counsel or perfect remedy....

Do not be troubled and do not fear. Trust strongly in me and have perfect hope in my mercy. When you think you are very far from me, I am often quite close to you; when you think all is lost, then the greater reward often follows. All is not lost, though some things happen contrary to your will. You should not judge of them according to your outward feeling, nor should you take any grief so sorely to heart that you do not have good hope to escape it. You should not think yourself wholly forsaken by me, though I send you for a time some grief and trouble, for this is the surer way to the kingdom of heaven.

Thomas à Kempis
The Imitation of Christ

> Don't say, "That person bothers me." Think, "That person sanctifies me."
>
> Blessed Josemaría Escrivá de Balaguer
> *The Way*

On conformity to the will of God in time of trial:

> Embrace with peace all things that are contrary to the senses in pains, sicknesses, affronts, contradictions, loss of property, the death of relatives or of other persons who are dear to us; and ... receive [these trials] each day when we awake as coming from God. Tribulations are those blessed treasuries in which the saints find such stores of merits. We cannot give greater glory to God than by conforming ourselves in all things to his holy will....
>
> Perfection consists in conforming ourselves to the will of God in those things which are disagreeable to us. The Venerable F. Avila says, "It is of more use to say once, 'Blessed be God,' in any contradiction, than to thank him six thousand times when we are pleased." We must also be conformed to those crosses which come to us by means of others ... because it all comes from God. Not that the Lord then wills the fault of the person who offends us, but he does will that we should be humble and mortified....
>
> We call tribulations evils and misfortunes, and we make them so by suffering them with impatience. But if we received them with resignation, they would become graces and jewels to enrich our crown in heaven. In a

word, he who is always united with the will of God is a saint and enjoys even here on earth a perpetual peace.

St. Alphonsus Liguori
The Great Means of Salvation and of Perfection

Lining up our thinking with God's thinking might help us see some good in painful circumstances. His plan is to bring us to holiness; his method is to conform us to his will, which may or may not include suffering.

Our greatest fault is that we wish to serve God in our own way, not in his way; according to our will, not according to his will. When he wishes us to be sick, we wish to be well; when he desires us to serve him by suffering, we desire to serve him by works; when he wishes us to exercise charity, we wish to exercise humility; when he seeks from us resignation, we wish for devotion, a spirit of prayer, or some other virtue.

And this is not because the things we desire may be more pleasing to him, but because they are more to our taste. This is certainly the greatest obstacle we can raise to our own perfection, for it is beyond doubt that if we wish to be saints according to our own will, we shall never be so at all. To be truly a saint, it is necessary to be one according to the will of God.

St. Francis de Sales
A Year With the Saints

Confession Leads to Freedom

The devil and his underlings can see the effort we make to rise above our fallen nature and live as God's sons, and they are continually attempting to frighten and discourage us by the unpleasant things that happen to us....

But we have someone living in us who is far stronger than our adversary. If we are at peace with God and if, with all our hearts, we say to the Father at every moment, "Thy will be done," we shall never be overcome. No attack will be able to vanquish us, no assault to hurt us. When we confess our sins and acknowledge our own guilt, when we refuse to give in to the urgings of our lower nature, we stir up against us the hostility of the instigator of all evil; but by freely surrendering our lives to the Lord we secure a peace with God that nothing can destroy.

If we claim the gift of his Spirit in order to choose what God wants and to reject what he prohibits, then a wonderful thing happens. We experience his power at work in us, and we find him taking over our struggles and finishing our battles for us.

Pope St. Leo the Great
The Binding of the Strong Man

The seventeenth century's St. Charles of Sezze experienced severe temptations and depression immediately upon entering the Franciscan Order. He had wanted to be a Franciscan for many years and so was dismayed, he said, by "the spirit of sadness that seemed to penetrate my very bones." This was more than the natural letdown one might expect after reaching a much-anticipated goal. He was filled with a "deep melancholy," "suffocated by anxiety," "abandoned and derelict" with no "freedom or the least bit of comfort." He was tempted to give up his vocation and return to the world, and he stewed privately over this for several weeks.

> How suddenly things had changed! Happiness into bitterness, joys into tears! I was as though beside myself with sadness, buried in a dark night of anxieties, with everything contributing to making my illness even worse. When I looked at the sun its very rays filled me with gloom; the birds with their songs only served to remind me of my affliction; everything I saw or heard made me sad....

Charles found the answer to his suffering in the sacrament of reconciliation. His conclusions are surprisingly modern—particularly the insight that secrecy depletes the spirit. His solution is easily applied to other situations, particularly those involving temptation.

> For two or three weeks I remained in this trouble without informing my confessor.... But as God planned it and helped me by his grace, I determined to tell him everything. I did so in confession. He listened very charitably, and my courage mounted. He gave me very good advice. I was never to keep any sort of temptation hidden, for in that way it only acquires greater strength and easily makes too great an impression....
>
> By talking this over with my confessor I was not thereby freed from the temptation to melancholy, since it lasted all during the novitiate year. Still, I was really greatly

strengthened.... I received a great help to keep going. In all this I noticed the power of the sacrament of penance for helping the Christian; it certainly strengthened me in overcoming these trials.

St. Charles of Sezze
Autobiography of St. Charles of Sezze

Total Surrender

I wish I could persuade spiritual persons that the way of perfection does not consist in many devices, nor in much cogitation, but in denying themselves completely, and yielding themselves to suffer everything for the love of Christ. And if there is failure in this exercise, all other methods of walking in the spiritual way are merely a beating about the bush, and profitless trifling, although a person should have a very high contemplation and communication with God.

St. John of the Cross
A Year With the Saints

A reflection on courage as a weapon against suffering:

To bear pain well is to meet it courageously, not to shrink or waver but to pray for God's help, then to look at it steadfastly, to summon what nerve we have of mind and body, to receive its attack, and to bear up against it (while strength is given us) as against some visible enemy in close combat.

Venerable Cardinal John Henry Newman
A Newman Treasury

Trust in God, who does nothing in vain.

God was all-complete, all-blessed in himself; but it was his will to create a world for his glory. He is almighty, and might have done all things himself, but it has been his will to bring about his purposes by the beings he has created....

Therefore, I will trust him.... If I am in sickness, my sickness may serve him; in perplexity, my perplexity may serve him; if I am in sorrow, my sorrow may serve him. My sickness, or perplexity, or sorrow may be necessary causes of some great end, which is quite beyond [my understanding]. He does nothing in vain;... he knows what he is about.

Venerable Cardinal John Henry Newman
A Newman Treasury

"Proof of the Living God"

Père Jacques—Lucien-Louis Bunel—died a victim of the Nazis, condemned for hiding three Jewish boys at his school near Paris. Père Jacques was a Carmelite priest, a member of the

French Resistance, and a friend and support to fellow inmates, from atheists to Catholics, at Mauthausen concentration camp.

In 1943, four months before his arrest, he gave a retreat for Carmelite nuns in which he focused on the meaning of suffering as reflected in the life of Christ. That he put his theology into practice was evident at Mauthausen. One of the inmates there, moved by the priest's kindness and courage, said "he was proof of the living God."

> If we only listened to Christ, who came to teach the world true happiness! Against true human happiness, there is, or appears to be, a great obstacle: the evil of suffering.
>
> There are two ways of dealing with suffering. The first way is to eliminate its causes by taking every precaution against it. When it does come, we try to whisk it away or suppress it by all the means at our disposal. However, there is a second way we can deal with suffering: we can "baptize" it.
>
> In general, most people adopt the first way.... They want to eliminate [suffering] by avoiding it, strangling it, brushing it aside....
>
> Christ knew that this way of dealing with suffering is simply a kind of stop-gap measure and does not strike the root of the evil. It can work only for a few hours, or days, or months. Christ adopted another way, a deeply divine, definitive way. Christ converted suffering into happiness.... Since [he] chose suffering for himself, suffering is not a curse or a plague to be avoided at any price. Christ welcomed the cross and even said, "He who wishes to come after me must take up his cross every day and follow in my footsteps" [Lk 9: 23]....

Through his suffering, Christ has redeemed the world.... Each of us, through our suffering, can personally participate in the work of redemption as well. What an honor! With what tender affection God treats us! He could redeem us without our efforts, but he did not wish to do so.

Père Jacques
Père Jacques: Resplendent in Victory

Absence, isolation: trials for your perseverance. Holy Mass, prayer, sacraments, sacrifices, Communion of the saints: weapons to conquer in the trial.

Blessed Josemaría Escrivá de Balaguer
The Way

Patience in the Fight

Patience and suffering are linked, like the riddle of the chicken and the egg. Which comes first? Patience is a necessary virtue enabling us to handle suffering, but suffering can also produce patience.

The man who will suffer only as much as seems good to him, who will accept suffering only from those he chooses, is not truly patient. The truly patient man does not consider from whom the suffering comes, whether from a superior, an equal, a subordinate, whether from someone who is good and holy or someone who is evil and unworthy. It doesn't matter how great the trial, how often it comes or who inflicts it—he accepts it gratefully from the hand of God and counts it a great gain. For with God nothing that we suffer for his sake, no matter how small, passes without reward.

Be prepared for the fight, then, if you want to achieve victory. You cannot obtain the crown of patience without a struggle, and if you refuse to suffer, you refuse the crown. If you want the crown, fight bravely and bear up patiently. There is no rest without labor and no victory without a fight.

Thomas à Kempis
adapted from *The Imitation of Christ*

Hold to patience in your hearts, my friends, and put it into action when the situation calls for it. Don't let any abusive word from your neighbor stir up hatred in you, and don't allow any loss of things that pass away to upset you. If you are steadfast in fearing the loss of those things that last forever, you will never take seriously the loss of those that pass away; if you keep your eyes fixed on the glory of our eternal recompense, you will not resent a temporal injury. You must bear with those who oppose you, but also love those who bear with you. Seek an eternal reward in return for your temporal losses.

St. Gregory the Great
Be Friends of God

St. John Chrysostom wrote from exile to his good friend Olympias, who was dejected over the trials endured by the church and by the general chaos of the times. His advice is encouraging and practical at the same time.

Don't let any of these things that are happening trouble you. Stop invoking the help of this or that person and running after shadows (for that's what human alliances are). Instead, call upon Jesus persistently, ... and in a moment of time, all these evils will be dissolved. If you have already called upon him and they haven't been dissolved, such is the way God works.... He doesn't put down evils at the outset but when they've grown to a head. When hardly any of the enemy's malice remains ungratified, God suddenly brings tranquillity and leads things to an unexpected settlement....

Do you see the abundant resources of God? His wisdom, his extraordinary power, his loving kindness, his care? Don't be dismayed or troubled but continue to thank God for everything, praising and invoking him, beseeching and imploring him. Even if countless troubles come upon you, if tempests are stirred up before your eyes, don't let any of these things disturb you. Our master is not baffled by the difficulty, even if everything is reduced to the extremity of ruin....

If he makes things which don't exist come into being,... how much more will he fix things that already exist.

St. John Chrysostom
adapted from *Nicene and Post-Nicene Fathers*

God Alone

Blessed Peter Favre found consolation in suffering by turning his thoughts to God.

> Feeling very much downcast and depressed amid the pain and bitterness of my soul,... I lifted up my soul a little to God, and all this then seemed to be nothing at all. But also that one thing, namely, just lifting up my thoughts, seemed to me my best remedy on such occasions. For when thoughts are lifted up to higher things, none of the darts that can be hurled at the soul either wound or affect it in any way; for these trifles—call them railing, call them flailing—do not reach so far; I mean, they do not rise all the way to the spirit thus lifted up in God, whose tent no flail comes near.
>
> Then raise up your mind without delay whenever some earthly thing—word or deed—influences your spirit, no matter whether it be toward human happiness or useless sadness.
>
> Bl. Peter Favre
>
> *The Spiritual Writings of Pierre Favre*

> The sign of the cross is the most terrible weapon against the devil. Thus the church wishes not only that we should have it continually in front of our minds to recall to us just what our souls are worth and what they cost Jesus Christ, but also that we should make it at every juncture ourselves; when we go to bed, when we awaken during the night, when we get up,... and above all, when we are tempted. We can say that a Christian who makes the sign of the

cross with genuine religious sentiments, that is to say, when fully aware of the action which he is performing, makes all hell tremble.

St. John Vianney
Sermons

Elisabeth Leseur suffered alone. She offers a remedy for others who lack the support of friends.

It is a suffering sent from God, which I offer to him, that I should have no one, among all my beloved friends, to whom I might open my heart and who might understand and help me.... When I want to pour out my soul, I go to [God], and whether at church or in the silence of my room, he brings me increase of strength and fills me with joy greater than any words can say. After all, perhaps he alone can penetrate to the infinite depth and sensitiveness of the soul.

Elisabeth Leseur
A Wife's Story

How can God refuse to protect us, if it is true that we never give him more glory than when we ask him to do so? No, he will never reject you. Whatever enemy persecutes you, whatever sorrow weighs you down, however weak you may find yourself, lean on God. Throw yourself boldly into his arms; he will never withdraw them and let you fall.

St. Claude de la Colombière
A Jesuit at the English Court

SIX

WHAT'S THE POINT? FINDING MEANING IN SUFFERING

The saints generally agree that suffering is a mystery, but they also agree that when it comes, it can serve a purpose. Elisabeth Leseur, a married woman who suffered heroically before her death in 1914, summed up the approach in her journal. On the one hand, suffering "is a great instrument ... of [personal] sanctification," she said. On the other hand, it can be offered as a prayer on behalf of others: "Our least sorrow ... can by divine action reach certain souls, whether near or far, and bring them light, peace, and holiness."

Leseur was married to Felix, a doctor and an atheist who not only reneged on his promise to let her practice her faith but actively attempted to subvert it. He succeeded. In 1896, seven years after their marriage, Elisabeth abandoned Catholicism. In an effort to push her from agnosticism into full atheism, Felix gave her the heretical *Life of Jesus* by Ernest Renan. Elisabeth, who was well educated and had an analytical mind, quickly discredited Renan's arguments. To Felix's dismay, she returned to the faith and developed a profound interior life of prayer and sacrifice.

Elisabeth maintained her warm affection for her husband and graciously fulfilled her role as a leader and hostess in their social circle. But the ill health that had plagued her since childhood gradually left her an invalid. She suffered atrociously at times from a long-standing intestinal abscess, liver ailments, breast cancer, and finally cancer throughout her body. The physical pain was exacerbated by her inability to share her deepest thoughts with Felix and by the spiritual isolation she felt as she carried out her social obligations among their mostly agnostic or atheistic friends. She kept up a cheerful attitude through it all and offered up her suffering specifically for Felix's conversion, as well as for the needs of others.

Elisabeth was forty-eight when she died in Felix's arms. Shortly after, he found her journal and other writings and was shattered to realize that, as he said, "she gave her life for me." "The eyes of my soul were opening little by little," he said, and three years later he became a Christian. In 1923 he was ordained a Dominican priest. Before his death in 1950, he succeeded in introducing Elisabeth's cause for canonization in Rome.

The quotes that follow reflect the experience of people like Elisabeth and Felix and many Christians trying to make sense out of life. The saints are generally tough-minded when considering the meaning to be found in suffering, and they don't offer any easy way out. They do help the suffering focus on the possible benefits inherent in what they endure.

Suffering Sanctifies

The example of Christ informs the Christian attitude toward suffering.

> It is when one suffers most that one sanctifies oneself and others. ... Jesus is not saving the world by his divine words, miracles, or blessings but by his cross. The most fruitful hour of his life was that of his greatest abasement and

prostration, when he was plunged deepest into suffering and humiliation.

Venerable Charles de Foucauld
Spiritual Autobiography of Charles de Foucauld

Blessed Henry Suso, a fourteenth-century mystic, referred to Christ as the Eternal Wisdom and to himself as the Servant. This dialogue, from *The Little Book of Eternal Wisdom,* explores the tension, pain, and ultimate benefit of suffering in Christian life.

Servant: Lord,... my sufferings are measureless, completely beyond my strength. Is there anyone in the world who has more painful and constant sufferings than I?... How am I to endure them? Lord, if you'd send me ordinary sufferings, I could bear them, but I don't see how I can endure such extraordinary trials as these....

Eternal Wisdom: All sick people imagine that their sickness is the worst, and all people in distress, that their distress is the greatest. If I had sent you other sufferings, you'd feel the same as you do now. Conform yourself freely to my will in whatever pain I ask you to bear, without trying to get out of one or another kind of suffering.... I want only what is best for you, ... and I know better than you what is for your own good....

Servant: Lord, it's easy to talk, but the reality is very difficult to endure. It's so painful!

Eternal Wisdom: If suffering didn't hurt, it couldn't be called suffering. There is nothing more painful than suffering and nothing more joyful than to have suffered. Suffering is a short pain and a long joy. Suffering gives the victim pain now and joy later. Suffering kills suffering....

Suffering is a reproach in the eyes of the world, but an honor before me. Suffering extinguishes my wrath and wins my favor.... It changes an earthly person into a heavenly one.... It diminishes pleasure and increases grace....

Those who know how profitable suffering is ought to receive it as a gift worthy of God. It has awakened many once destined for eternal death—plunged into profound sleep—and directed them to a good life.... It keeps the soul humble and teaches patience.... Everyone benefits from suffering, whether in a state of sin, on the eve of conversion, in the fulness of grace, or on the summit of perfection. It takes away sin, lessens the fires of purgatory, drives out temptation, consumes imperfections, and renews the spirit....

People who haven't suffered, what do they know?... I would just as soon create suffering out of nothing than leave my friends without its benefits. In suffering, every virtue is preserved, humanity adorned, our neighbor reformed, and God praised.... All the saints are on the side of the suffering for they have walked the same path. They call out to those in pain that their ordeals contain no poison but rather are like a wholesome beverage. Patience in suffering is better than raising the dead or working other miracles. It is a narrow way that leads directly to heaven. It makes us companions of the martyrs, carries honor with it, and leads us to victory against every enemy....

In short, the world regards those who suffer as poor. I regard them as blessed for they are my chosen.

Blessed Henry Suso
adapted from *The Little Book of Eternal Wisdom*

Place a nail on a board. Will it ever go through the wood on its own, no matter how sharp it is? No, indeed. You will only sink it into the board by hitting it with a hammer. We are just the same; it is only by hammer-blows that God manages to humble us, no matter how good our native disposition might be.

St. Anthony Claret
Mystic and Man of Action

Abundant Fruit

St. Basil finds many benefits in suffering. He promises that God will never abandon those in pain.

If you are a good Christian, you should be pleased if you suffer troubles, since you will become more worthy. And if you are a sinner, you should be pleased if you are afflicted, for in this way you will be cleansed of your sins and will find consolation in the time to come. Affliction offers benefits in each case....

If a sinner is rebuked by God but refuses to change old ways, merely despairing for life, and saying, "I have no chance of being pardoned, God has abandoned me, my whole life is heading for disaster...," such a person signs a death warrant and falls on the sword of desperation, joining the group denounced by the prophet when he says, "You have rebuked them and yet they show no remorse, you have punished them and yet they ignore the warning."

But you should do everything ... to avoid becoming one of that group.... Even though the punishment may seem harsh at the time, it ... will steer you away from sin and lead you to virtue....

Anyone who keeps [his] mind on God will never be without him. He will soothe the pains of your body and strengthen its capacity to endure; and even if your body is covered with festering wounds, you will be able to retain your mental composure and balance, with the help of our Lord, Jesus Christ.

St. Basil
Gateway to Paradise

One ounce of the cross is worth more than a million pounds of prayer. One day of crucifixion is worth more than a hundred years of all other exercises. It is worth more to remain a moment on the cross, than to taste the delights of paradise.

Venerable Maria Vittoria Angelini
A Year With the Saints

Knowledge of God comes through testing and trials.

Those who want to be enlarged, elevated, extended, consoled, and increased in God must first be well tried and tested in what they are; in body and in spirit they must suffer restrictions, curbs, humiliations, restraints, griefs, diminishment, and so on. For it is through the mortification of one's own flesh and the abnegation of one's own spirit that one is led on to the possession of God. Through the narrow gate must entry be made; and that narrow gate ... is the way that leads on to the heart, and those who have returned to the heart enter into truth and life.

Bl. Peter Favre
The Spiritual Writings of Pierre Favre

We must feel the weight of the cross, otherwise there is no merit.

St. Joseph Moscati
Saints in the Making

Suffering spares us self-delusion.

When a man's spirits are high, he is pleased with everything; and with himself especially. He can act with vigor and promptness, and he mistakes this mere constitutional energy for strength of faith. He is cheerful and contented; and he mistakes this for Christian peace. And, if happy in his family, he mistakes mere natural affection for Christian benevolence, and the confirmed temper of Christian love. In short, he is in a dream, from which nothing could have saved him except deep humility, and nothing will ordinarily rescue him except sharp affliction.

Venerable Cardinal John Henry Newman
A Newman Treasury

> Suffer the burden of dryness in the realization that you will now better know whether or not you are master of yourself. It's no great accomplishment to conquer and rule ourselves when we feel fervently that we are near to Christ. [Rather] we recognize ... the really true victory and effective rule over ourselves at that very time when our King seems far away from us.
>
> Bl. Peter Favre
> adapted from *To the Other Towns*

To Be Like Christ

Edith Stein (Sr. Teresa Benedicta of the Cross) was a Carmelite nun of Jewish descent. She died at Auschwitz concentration camp at the hands of the Nazis. Stein had offered herself to God in voluntary suffering—expiatory suffering—in imitation of Jesus, who died to reconcile humanity to God. In an essay written in honor of the feast of St. John of the Cross, she spoke of the role of atoning suffering in the life of the Christian.

> When someone desires to suffer, it is not merely a pious reminder of the suffering of the Lord. Voluntary expiatory suffering is what truly and really unites one to the Lord intimately. When it arises it comes from an already existing relationship with Christ. For, by nature, a person flees from suffering. And the mania for suffering caused by a perverse lust for pain differs completely from the desire to suffer in expiation. Such lust is not a spiritual striving,

but a sensory longing, no better than other sensory desires, in fact worse, because it is contrary to nature.

Only someone whose spiritual eyes have been opened to the supernatural correlations of worldly events can desire suffering in expiation, and this is only possible for people in whom the spirit of Christ dwells....

But because *being* one with Christ is our sanctity, and progressively *becoming* one with him our happiness on earth, the love of the cross in no way contradicts being a joyful child of God. Helping Christ carry his cross fills one with a strong and pure joy.... Those who have a predilection for the way of the cross by no means deny that Good Friday is past and that the work of salvation has been accomplished....

To suffer and to be happy although suffering,... to walk on the dirty and rough paths of this earth and yet to be enthroned with Christ at the Father's right hand,... this is the life of the Christian until the morning of eternity breaks forth.

St. Edith Stein
The Collected Works

Our suffering works mysteriously, first in ourselves by a kind of renewal, and also in others, perhaps far away, without our ever knowing what we are accomplishing. Suffering is an action. Christ on the cross has perhaps done more for humanity than Christ speaking and acting in Galilee or Jerusalem. Suffering creates life; it transforms all that it touches.

Elisabeth Leseur
A Wife's Story

> Christianity is based on sacrifice. Each Christian in his own hour should imitate Christ and amid men's indifference make his sacrifice, to be joined to that of the Master. He should know Gethsemane or Calvary in the degree that his strength can support. He should offer himself as oblation for the salvation of all, and stretch out his arms to the cross in supplication for all. His lips should proclaim him a follower of the crucified, and his soul should give its utmost purity for sinners and the disinherited.
>
> Elisabeth Leseur
> *A Wife's Story*

The Way to God

In the Gospel of Matthew, Jesus tells his followers to "take my yoke upon you ... for my yoke is easy, and my burden light" (Mt 11:29). In a sermon on that passage, Cardinal Newman stressed the difficulties entailed in living as a Christian and the necessity of coming to Christ through suffering.

> Let us set it down then, as a first principle in religion, that all of us must come to Christ, in some sense or other, through things naturally unpleasant to us; it may be even through bodily suffering, such as the apostles endured, or it may be nothing more than the subduing of our natural infirmities and the sacrifice of our natural wishes. It may be pain greater or pain less, on a public stage or a private one.

But, till the words "yoke" and "cross" can stand for something pleasant, the bearing of our yoke and cross is something not pleasant; and though rest is promised as our reward, yet the way to rest must lie through discomfort and distress of heart....

I do not of course mean, far from it, that religion is not full of joy and peace also: "My yoke," says Christ, "is easy, and my burden is light." But grace makes it so. In itself it is severe, and any form of doctrine which teaches otherwise forgets that Christ calls us to his yoke, and that yoke is a cross.

Venerable Cardinal John Henry Newman
Parochial and Plain Sermons

You need crosses to make you think of God.

St. John Vianney
Sermons

SEVEN

LOOKING BEYOND OUR PAIN: AT THE SERVICE OF OTHERS

None of the saints achieved holiness by battening down the hatches against disruptive humanity. All of them were dedicated to easing the suffering of others, either through prayer (those saints in the cloister, or otherwise restricted) or through hands-on help (those in the world).

Dorothy Day, who died in 1980 and whose cause for canonization is in process, exemplified this in a very contemporary way. After a tumultuous youth that included numerous affairs, a short-lived marriage, an abortion, a common-law marriage, and the birth of her daughter, Day converted to Catholicism. A writer and intellectual, she had been committed to the poor prior to her conversion; her entry into the church helped focus her thinking. With Peter Maurin, a French Catholic activist, she cofounded the Catholic Worker Movement in New York City to address the needs of the homeless, the hungry, the mentally ill, the working poor—any and all on the margins of society.

Day and Maurin established houses of hospitality where they fed the hungry and sheltered the homeless; started a newspaper, *The Catholic Worker,* to bring a Christian perspective to issues of social justice; and lived and worked in poverty themselves along with the dedicated staff who joined the venture. "We never expected to solve the nation's problems," Dorothy wrote, "but we thought we ought to try to do all that we could do and,...

well, a step would have been taken and that's what I thought the Lord wanted from us—as many steps as we could manage."

To these traditional and socially acceptable works of mercy, Day added others that were more challenging to the status quo. She was a pacifist, even during World War II, a stand that cost her many supporters. As an ardent activist on behalf of civil rights, she was shot at, shadowed by the FBI, and arrested. She joined picket lines and was arrested for supporting strikes calling for a just wage for workers.

Day often said, "Love is the measure by which we shall be judged," and her deeds matched her belief. Christ "made heaven hinge on the way we act toward him in his disguise of commonplace, frail, ordinary humanity," she wrote. Referring to the twenty-fifth chapter of the Gospel of Matthew, Day asked: "Did you give me food when I was hungry? Did you give me to drink when I was thirsty? Did you give me clothes when my own were all in rags? Did you come to see me when I was sick, or in prison or in trouble?

"And to those who say, aghast, that they never had a chance to do such a thing, that they lived two thousand years too late, he will say again what they had the chance of knowing all their lives, that if these things were done for the very least of his brethren, they were done to him."

Christ Is for All

Blessed Peter Favre, one of the first Jesuits, was known as a gentle, lovable, congenial man. He was especially sensitive to the sufferings of humanity, as is evident in the following.

I rose at three in the morning...to pray for my neighbors in their needs.... There passed before my mind's eye the different kinds of human suffering, men's weaknesses, sins, obstinacy, despair, sorrow, death, as well as the famines, the plagues, the other burdens they endure. Then there came to me the thought of Christ the Redeemer, Christ the Consoler, Christ the Lord God. I prayed to him by the power of all these titles of his that he deign to give help... to all....

I also felt the desire and prayed with intense... feeling that I be given the grace to be the servant of Christ the Consoler, Christ the Helper, Christ the Rescuer, the Liberator, the Enricher, the Strengthener, and that through him I might be able to give aid, to console, rescue from all sorts of danger, strengthen the many who are in need....

Bl. Peter Favre
To the Other Towns

St. Eugene de Mazenod considered everyone of infinite worth since all, he said, "have been ransomed by God made man." Accordingly, he dedicated himself to the needy of his hometown, Aix, in France. Along with his practical care of the poor he provided spiritual assistance, and in 1813 he preached a series of sermons specifically for them. The city's high society was indignant but de Mazenod was not deterred. In his first sermon he rallied his poverty-stricken congregation with the following words.

The world considers you the scum of society.... That is what the world thinks. That is what you are in its eyes.... Come now, and learn from us what you are in the eyes of faith.

You, the poor of Jesus Christ, the afflicted and the wretched, the sick and suffering, those covered with sores—all of you whom misery overwhelms. My brethren, my dear brethren, my respectable brethren, listen to me.

You are the children of God, the brothers and sisters of Jesus Christ, the coheirs of his eternal kingdom, the cherished portion of his inheritance; you are, in the words of St. Peter, the holy nation, you are kings, you are priests, you are, yes, in a certain way, gods....

So lift up your heads! Let your dejected spirit rise!... Let your eyes look inward.... There, within you, is an immortal soul, created to the image of God, ... a soul redeemed at the cost of the blood of Jesus Christ.... Therefore, O Christians, recognize your dignity.

St. Eugene de Mazenod
Living in the Spirit's Fire

Spiritual Riches

Dorothy Day, who spent her life doing corporal works of mercy, illustrates here the importance of the spiritual works of mercy.

It made me happy that I could be with my mother the last few weeks of her life, and for the last ten days at her bedside daily and hourly. Sometimes I thought to myself that it was like being present at a birth to sit by a dying person and see their intentness on what is happening to them. It almost seems that one is absorbed in a struggle, a fearful, grim, physical struggle, to breathe, to swallow, to live.

And so, I kept thinking to myself, how necessary it is for one of their loved ones to be beside them, to pray for them, to offer up prayers for them unceasingly, as well as to do all those little offices one can. When my daughter was a tiny little girl, she said to me once, "When I get to be a great big woman and you are a little tiny girl, I'll take care of you." And I thought of that when I had to feed my mother by the spoonful and urge her to eat her custard.

How good God was to me, to let me be there. I had prayed so constantly that I would be beside her when she died; for years I had offered up that prayer. And God granted it quite literally. I was there, holding her hand, and she just turned her head and sighed. That was her last breath, that little sigh; and her hand was warm in mine for a long time after.

Dorothy Day
On Pilgrimage

Christians are supposed to help meet the needs of the lonely, the depressed, the poor, the ill—all who are impoverished in some way. Charles de Foucauld points out that in these, the Christian meets Jesus.

We must no longer live for ourselves but for our neighbor, who is Jesus. We must forget about ourselves, which is the first thing that Jesus wants from his disciples. Not only must we do good to others at certain times, but we must never let a chance to do good to a neighbor pass by without acting on it.

Neglect is serious, for it is Jesus whom we neglect to save! It is not enough to give to those who ask, we must give to those who need. Every time we do not give spiritual or material aid to someone who needs it, it is Jesus whom we are neglecting to help! We must organize our lives according to our calling, in order to do the best possible good to all those within reach of our spiritual and temporal action, in order to not commit this terrible, painful neglect of Jesus.

And we must try with all the means within our power to extend this spiritual and material action as far as possible, to help Jesus as much as possible, to reach him as far as possible, to comfort him to the greatest extent, in as many beings as possible.

Venerable Charles de Foucauld
Scriptural Meditations on Faith

A Heroic Response to Suffering

Titus Brandsma, a native of the Netherlands and a Carmelite priest, was sixty years old when arrested for his resistance to the Nazis. A university professor, theologian, and mystic, he had for years condemned Nazism as "a black lie." As a representative of the Catholic bishops of the Netherlands, he opposed all directives aimed at persecuting Jews and silencing the church.

When the Gestapo picked up Fr. Brandsma for his resistance,

he was not in good health. Nevertheless, over the six months of his imprisonment until his death at Dachau in 1942, he ignored his own pain and worked to ease the suffering of his fellow inmates. Many considered him "the friendliest man in the camp," one inmate later said, and the younger prisoners called him "Uncle Titus." He took care of the sick, heating stones in the stove to place in their beds for warmth and, in a small gesture of comfort, tucking them in. He heard confessions, prayed with and counseled men as they walked around the compound, and held prayer services.

Fr. Brandsma closed his Sunday service with a moving ritual, a sort of spiritual communion in which he approached each man, looked directly at him, and said, "The body of our Lord Jesus Christ keep your soul unto life everlasting." In the morning and evening, when inmates came to ask his blessing, he shook their hands while silently tracing the sign of the cross there. He carried out this ministry, which was strictly forbidden by the Nazis, under constant threat of death.

"He was a guardian angel to me," one prisoner said. "When I felt depressed, he tapped me on the shoulder and said, 'Just remember that God is good. He must have a plan for you. He feels that you are worthy of making this sacrifice.'" But the priest was also a realist. When some of the inmates complained about particularly brutal guards, Titus recommended they pray for them. When the prisoners replied that that was difficult, he said, "You don't have to pray for them all day long."

The Nazis, angered by Titus' calm demeanor, frequently beat him and left him nearly unconscious in the dirt. Other inmates rescued him and carried him to the barracks. One of these, a Polish priest, said that he was "so even-tempered and approachable,... so cheerful in the midst of disaster,... that he deeply touched our hearts."

Finally, suffering from uremic poisoning and a severe foot infection, Titus ended up in the dreaded camp hospital. There, doctors performed barbaric experiments on him before ordering his death by lethal injection.

Even then, Titus remained concerned with the needs of others. In a conversation with the nurse who attended him, he discovered she was a fallen-away Catholic. She had left the church because of "bad priests," she said. Titus told her to observe the good conduct of the priests in the camp and added that he himself was happy to suffer for God's sake. He gave her his rosary, and when she said she had forgotten the prayers, he told her: "Surely you can still say, 'Pray for us sinners.'"

The nurse administered the lethal dose on July 26, 1942. After the war she returned to the faith and later testified to Titus Brandsma's final moments.

> It is the hour for prayer; if you hear the poor calling you, mortify yourselves and leave God for God.
>
> St. Vincent de Paul
> *Monsieur Vincent*

In her book *The Long Loneliness*, Dorothy Day described some of the thinking that motivated those involved with the Catholic Worker Movement.

> Every one of us who was attracted to the poor had a sense of guilt, of responsibility, a feeling that in some way we were living on the labor of others. The fact that we were born in a certain environment, were enabled to go to school, were endowed with the ability to compete with others and hold our own, that we had few physical dis-

abilities—all these things marked us as the privileged in some way. We felt a respect for the poor and destitute as those nearest to God....

[Christ] was born in a stable.... He did not come to be a temporal king.... He worked with his hands, spent the first years of his life in exile, and the rest of his early manhood in a crude carpenter shop in Nazareth.... He trod the roads in his public life, and the first men he called were fishermen, small owners of boats and nets. He was familiar with the migrant worker and the proletariat, and some of his parables dealt with them....

He directed his sublime words to the poorest of the poor, to the people who thronged the towns,... who hung around, sick and poverty-stricken, at the doors of rich men.

He had set us an example, and the poor and destitute were the ones we wished to reach.... We did not feel that Christ meant we should remain silent in the face of injustice and accept it even though he had said, "The poor you shall always have with you."

Dorothy Day
The Long Loneliness

The early church fathers frequently and forcefully reminded Christians of their duty to ease the suffering of the poor. St. John Chrysostom once preached regarding wealthy women, fond of jewels: "Christ will make you pay the price for those pearls and bring the poor who have perished with hunger into our midst." In the following sermon, he advances the same theme, although with more restraint.

Would you honor the body of Christ? Do not despise his nakedness. Do not honor him here in church, clothed in silk vestments, and then pass him by unclothed and frozen outside. Remember that he who said, "This is my body" and made good his words, also said, "You saw me hungry and gave me no food and insofar as you did it not to one of these, you did it not to me."

God has no need of golden vessels but of golden hearts. I am not saying that you should not give golden altar vessels and so on, but I am insisting that nothing can take the place of almsgiving....

Consider that Christ is that tramp who comes in need of a night's lodging. You turn him away and then start laying rugs on the floor and draping the walls, hanging lamps on silver chains on the columns. Meanwhile the tramp is locked up in prison and you never give him a glance. Well, again, I am not condemning munificence in these matters. Make your house beautiful, by all means, but also look after the poor, or rather, look after the poor first....

Adorn your house, if you will, but do not forget your brother in distress. He is a temple of infinitely greater value.

St. John Chrysostom
Deep Down Things: Burning Love for the Poor

Men live only on the surface of their souls. If we knew how to withdraw into ourselves and understood the meaning and use of suffering, then at the least sign from some other soul we should know its grief or tenderness and pour light into it and make it live.

Elisabeth Leseur
A Wife's Story

EIGHT

IS GOD PAYING ATTENTION? CARRYING THE CROSS ASSIGNED US

Even the saints sometimes had a hard time believing that God actually cared about them. Was he aware that the suffering in their lives could seem interminable or was badly timed from the start? The whole notion that "God's timing is always perfect," as St. Leo the Great said, or that he chooses the crosses we bear, as St. Francis de Sales claimed, seems farfetched. Sometimes saints, wriggling under the weight of these truths, challenged them.

St. John Vianney, the Curé of Ars, for example, couldn't quite accept the fact that God would nail him to the cross of the remote, depressing village of Ars for year upon endless year. "They leave me here like a dog on a leash," he said of his superiors. What Vianney wanted was solitude and the time, he said, to weep over his "poor sins." What he got, at Ars, was about two thousand visitors a week and sixteen hours a day in the confessional.

As word of his remarkable skill as a confessor spread, waves of penitents flooded the village, and Vianney looked for a way out. Some priests, jealous of his success, circulated a petition demanding his removal. Vianney somehow got hold of it and signed it himself. When that failed, he ran away—not once but three times, the last at the age of sixty-five. Each time his parishioners persuaded him to return until, after the last bid for freedom, he bowed to the inevitable. In all, Vianney spent over forty years at Ars.

So this was God's idea of the appropriate length of time for Vianney to bear his suffering: a lifetime. And God's expression of his personal interest in and care for Vianney? To deny him what he wanted the most in order to give him what would serve others the best.

The truth is that no time is a good time to suffer. Nevertheless, the saints suggest in the following quotes that not only does God meet us in the particular pain we bear, he also gives us the strength to bear it. He does provide relief when he judges the moment is right. For some, that moment might be nothing more than a respite before another wave of suffering or, as in the case of Vianney, the relief may come only at death. The saints imply that the person reconciled to the will of God will see his hand in the circumstances, and find that enough.

> However hard life may be, however long our days of sadness,... we must never seek to leave the foot of the cross sooner than God would have us do.
>
> Venerable Charles de Foucauld
> *Spiritual Autobiography of Charles de Foucauld*

Waiting on God

Sometimes we ask ourselves why the Lord makes us wait so long for an answer to our prayers. If his love for us is so great, how is it that he does not heal us straightaway when we turn to him for help?

This question has been asked in every generation. It is the universal cry of the human heart, voiced by the psalmist when he complained, "How long, O Lord, will you forget me?" (Ps 13:1), and by the martyrs in the Book of Revelation lying slain beneath the altar (Rv 6:9-10). But just as Job had to learn how limited was his knowledge of the mind of God, so we too must realize that as high as the heavens are above the earth, so high are the Lord's ways above our ways and the Lord's thoughts above our thoughts (Is 55:9).

His vision of our situation includes factors that are hidden from us. We see only our present need, but his eyes range ahead over the whole of our lives, and not of ours only, but of all those other lives which are affected by ours. He sees the deep needs of each one of us and of the whole of mankind ... God's timing is always perfect.

Pope St. Leo the Great
The Binding of the Strong Man

I begin to understand what St. Paul meant when he said, "I long to depart this life and be with Christ" [Phil 1:23]. Not that I dare believe or suggest that I've suffered enough. No, I'm only beginning. But I feel it will be sweet one day to die after having calmly and courageously accepted my small portion of the cross and carried it ... to the end determined by him. I feel the weight and burden of the cross imposed on me ... but I didn't choose it myself. God—I cannot and will not oppose him—chose it, and it is only right that I persevere. He who chose this cross will give me the strength to carry it as long as it is his will.

Blessed Mary Frances Schervier
Mother Frances Schervier:
A Sketch of Her Life and Character

> If we want to follow Christ, we must never desert penance and the cross. Like him, we must persevere until the Spirit tells us "that we may rest from our labors" [Rv 14:13]. On the cross we must remain until we are taken down by the hands of another. We must not descend from it through our own negligence [of the will of God].
>
> St. Bernard of Clairvaux
> in *Mother Frances Schervier: A Sketch of Her Life and Character*

Jesus' Cross and Ours

God cares for us enough to have become one of us, experiencing our weakness and fears from the inside. St. Leo the Great reminds us that at the moment of our greatest fear, God is by our side, supporting us.

> Jesus trembled with fear in the Garden of Gethsemane; he was so afraid that he sweated blood, and he made no attempt to conceal it.... Thousands of angels could have rallied to his support and wiped out his enemies, but he preferred the experience of our fears to the exercise of his mighty power.
>
> This was the way the Lord chose to save us, the way he saw in his wisdom to be the best. The first to understand it was Peter, the apostle who had panicked in the face of the mob which came to arrest his master and who had

denied him like a coward.... It was because the Lord had himself been afraid first that Peter was able to repent of his cowardice and be restored to the rocklike firmness of a true member of Christ's body. Unless death's divine conqueror had been afraid, Peter could never have conquered his human fears.

But as he stood quaking in the courtyard of the High Priest amid the slanders,... the lies,... the blows and spitting, Peter's frightened eyes were met by eyes that had foreseen his terror. At that moment the Lord looked upon him with a gaze that penetrated his very heart. It was as if Jesus said to him: "Do not be afraid. This is the time of my ordeal, yours has not yet come. You too will overcome. I know your weakness from the inside; I was afraid for your sake. Do not be ashamed of your fears, for I have shared them. Have confidence in me; you too will overcome."

St. Leo the Great
The Binding of the Strong Man

In a letter to St. Jane de Chantal, St. Francis de Sales writes that the crosses we bear are tailored to our need.

You are quite willing to have a cross, but you want to choose what sort it is to be; you want an ordinary cross, a bodily cross, or some other. And what is that, my beloved daughter? Ah no, I want your cross and mine to be no other than Jesus Christ's cross, both as regards its choice and the way it is laid upon us.

God knows very well what he is about and why; it is all for our good, you may be sure. God gave David the choice of the rod with which he should be scourged [2 Sm 24:12-14]; and it seems to me (blessed be God) that I would rather not have chosen, but left it all to his Divine Majesty. The more wholly a cross comes from God, the more we ought to love it.

St. Francis de Sales
Selected Letters

Sometimes people are so worried about their sins or so certain that God doesn't care about them that they reject him. St. John Chrysostom points out that God's care extends to everyone, regardless of the situation.

When the Lord called you it was not to settle a score against you, nor to bring you to account for your sins. It was to save you, to forgive you, to offer you new life. In the Gospel Jesus himself calls out to the whole human race: "Come to me, all you who are weary and overburdened, and I will give you rest. Take my yoke on your shoulders and learn to imitate me, for I am meek and humble of heart; then you will find rest for your souls" (Mt 11:28-29).

What an invitation! Come to me, all of you! Not just the powerful, the affluent, the educated, the strong, the healthy, the respectable; but also the weak, the poor, the underprivileged, the sick, the blind, the lame, the disabled, the hopeless, the abandoned. The Master makes no distinction between any of you; the good news is for everyone. Come to me, he says, all you who toil and groan under your burdens. He is interested especially in those who have squandered their lives, who are weighed down by their sins, who are filled with shame and no longer have any self-respect. These are the ones he calls to himself, not to punish them but to comfort their sorrows and ease their heavy load.

St. John Chrysostom
From Darkness to Light

NINE

BIG OR SMALL, IT'S STILL THE CROSS: THE ORDINARY SUFFERING OF DAILY LIFE

There was once a humble Trappist monk, Joseph Cassant, who was, perhaps, more humble than most. He had no particular intellectual gifts and, in fact, very few natural gifts at all. "He was meant to be a priest and a saint," Thomas Merton said of him in his book *The Waters of Siloe,* but "there seemed to be an infinite number of obstacles in his way." Cassant was in poor health and had tremendous difficulty passing the necessary academic exams for the priesthood. But "the greatest obstacle to his sanctity [lay] in what we today would call an 'inferiority complex.' He was keenly sensitive of his lack of gifts."

Cassant was attracted to the spiritual heroics he read about in the lives of the saints and could see around him in the lives of some of his fellow monks. His spiritual director wisely helped him understand that he would find holiness, instead, in accepting his weaknesses and devoting himself to living everyday life as perfectly as he could. He took to this advice with a zeal reflected in his notes: "If I can't find time for my studies or haven't got the brains, I will always do the will of Jesus without worrying about the future." "It doesn't do you any good to conquer your body [through rigorous penance] if you still feel anger in you."

Cassant was ordained a priest but died shortly after in 1903. The Trappists recognized him as such a saintly man that they introduced his cause for canonization in Rome, not those of other monks who led more spectacular spiritual lives.

Fr. Cassant was a contemporary of St. Thérèse of Lisieux, who also found sanctity in bearing perfectly the trials of ordinary life. Her "little way" to holiness is familiar to most Catholics, with its emphasis on thwarting self-will and making a loving response in the smallest difficulties of life.

The examples of Cassant and Thérèse are relevant for all Christians, because most of the time, as the saints point out in the following quotations, life consists of ordinary suffering lived out day to day. This is the field on which we are tested. The little crosses can be as effective as the big crosses in accomplishing God's work.

> It is no little thing for us to endure those sorrows God sends us day by day.
>
> St. Philip Neri
> *The Life of St. Philip Neri*

Minor Afflictions

Take advantage of little sufferings even more than of great ones. God considers not so much what we suffer as how we suffer. To suffer a great deal but badly is to suffer like the damned; to suffer much even bravely, but for an evil cause, is to suffer as a disciple of the devil; to suffer little or much for God's sake is to suffer like a saint....

Do what a shopkeeper does in regard to his business; turn everything to profit.... Even though it be only an insect sting or a pin-prick, a little eccentricity of your neighbor or some unintentional slight, the loss of some money, some

> little anxiety, a little bodily weariness, or a slight pain in your limbs. Turn everything to profit, as the grocer does in his shop, and you will soon become rich before God, just as the grocer becomes rich in money by adding penny to penny in his till. At the least annoyance say, "Thank you, Lord, your will be done." Then store up in God's memory bank, so to speak, the profitable cross you have just gained, and think no more about it except to repeat your thanks.

St. Louis de Montfort
God Alone

St. Teresa of Avila advised her nuns to quit complaining about the small inconveniences and illnesses of life. She wasn't speaking of serious illness, she said, but of those "minor indispositions which you may have and still keep going without worrying everybody else to death over them."

> Do not think of complaining about [your] weaknesses and minor ailments.... They come and go; and unless you get rid of the habit of talking about them and complaining of everything (except to God), you will never come to the end of them.... Think how many poor people there must be who are ill and have no one to complain to, for poverty and self-indulgence make bad company.... Learn to suffer a little for the love of God without telling everyone about it.

St. Teresa of Avila
The Letters of St. Teresa

Many people make a mistake because they prepare themselves only for major afflictions and remain totally without defense when it comes to small ones. Major afflictions rarely happen; little ones come up every day: the inconveniences encountered from the moods of those I am with or the pressing spiritual demands which my work brings me and which arise a hundred times a day.

St. Francis de Sales
www.inlink.com

One Man's Daily Cross

Venerable Francis Libermann is considered the second founder of the Congregation of the Holy Ghost. Libermann, a gentle, sensitive man, found his administrative duties oppressive. In a letter to a fellow priest, he revealed the small but crucifying sufferings of his day-to-day life and his determination to do the will of God in spite of the difficulties. His reflections will resonate with those who put up with the daily aggravations of a troubled marriage or unrewarding job or other painful circumstance.

Ever since God thrust me into this business, I haven't had a moment's consolation. My soul seems to have lost its receptivity for anything agreeable or consoling, but at the same time it has become highly sensitive to painful experiences.

Divine Providence certainly hasn't spared me in this respect....

I, with my great abhorrence and almost insurmountable repugnance for public relations, find myself thrust into the middle of things. I, who have difficulty even in talking to people, have to chatter away constantly. From morning till night I am tied up in giving direction....

It seems that everything in me rebels at staying here.... Nonetheless, I feel it would be criminal to entertain the thought [of leaving] even for an instant. God has bound me hand and foot to this crucifying but beloved work. I am quite convinced that, in order to obey the mighty Will that binds me, I must give up rest, satisfaction, and happiness....

I beg God to forgive my maladjustment and submit with all my heart to the Divine Will that holds me so tight it nearly strangles me. I believe I can honestly say I've never made a move to loosen the irons that God has clamped on me.... It's better for me to ... work for the salvation of so many ... than [abandon] the pathway traced out for me by his will.

Venerable Francis Libermann
A Light to the Gentiles

It is the little crosses that are our whole joy. They are more common than the big ones and prepare the heart to receive the latter when this is the will of our good Master.

St. Thérèse of Lisieux
The Story of a Soul

Some, guarded against great temptations, are frequently overcome by small ones in order that, humbled by their weakness in small trials, they may not presume on their own strength in great ones.

Thomas à Kempis
The Imitation of Christ

Little Conquests

You must be ready to suffer many great afflictions for the Lord, even martyrdom itself. Resolve to give him whatever you hold dearest if it pleases him to take it—father, mother, brother, husband, wife, child, your very eyes and life.... However, as long as Divine Providence does not send you such great, piercing afflictions,... bear patiently the slight injuries, the little inconveniences, the inconsequential losses that daily come to you.

By means of such trifles as these, borne with love and affection, you will completely win his heart and make it all your own. These little daily acts of charity, this headache, toothache or cold, this bad humor in a husband or wife, this broken glass, this contempt or that scorn, this loss of a pair of gloves, ring, or handkerchief, the little inconveniences incurred by going to bed early and getting up early to pray or receive Holy Communion, that little feeling of shame one has in performing certain acts of devotion in public—in short, all such little trials when accepted and embraced with love are highly pleasing to God's mercy. For a single cup of water God has promised to his faithful a sea of perfect bliss. Since such opportunities present themselves from moment to moment, it will be a great means of storing up vast spiritual riches if you only use them well.

Great opportunities to serve God rarely present themselves, but little ones are frequent.

St. Francis de Sales
Introduction to the Devout Life

See to it that you conquer yourself in little things if you would conquer in great things.

St. Philip Neri
Life of St. Philip Neri

TEN

CONSOLATION IN TRIAL: PRAYERS AND MEDITATIONS

The Pillar of the Cloud

Lead, Kindly Light, amid the encircling gloom,
   Lead Thou me on!
The night is dark, and I am far from home—
   Lead Thou me on!
Keep Thou my feet; I do not ask to see
The distant scene—one step enough for me.

I was not ever thus, nor prayed that Thou
   Shouldst lead me on.
I loved to choose and see my path, but now
   Lead Thou me on!
I loved the garish day, and, spite of fears,
Pride rules my will: remember not past years.

So long Thy power hath blest me, sure it still
   Will lead me on,
O'er moor and fen, o'er crag and torrent, till
   The night is gone;
And with the morn those angel faces smile
Which I have loved long since, and lost awhile.

Venerable Cardinal John Henry Newman
Verses on Various Occasions

Prayer to Ask of God the Virtue of Hope

My God, who has allowed us human hopes,
but who alone bestows Christian and
supernatural hope,
grant, I beseech you, by your grace,
this virtue to my soul, to the souls of all I love,
and to all Christian souls.
Let it enlighten and transform our lives,
our suffering, and even our death,
and let it uphold in us,
through the disappointment and sadness of each day,
an inner strength and unalterable serenity.

Elisabeth Leseur
A Wife's Story

Prayer to the Heart of Jesus

Does our life become from day to day more painful,
more oppressive, more replete with sufferings?
Blessed be he a thousand times who desires it so.
If life be harder, love makes it also stronger,
and only this love, grounded on suffering,
can carry the cross of my Lord, Jesus Christ.

I believe, O Lord, but strengthen my faith....
Heart of Jesus, I love you, but increase my love.
Heart of Jesus, I trust in you,
but give greater vigor to my confidence.

Heart of Jesus, I give my heart to you,
but so enclose it in you that it may never be separated from you.
Heart of Jesus, I am all yours....
even unto the complete sacrifice of my life.

Blessed Miguel Pro
www.ewtn.com

Consolation

When I sink down in gloom or fear,
Hope blighted or delay'd,
Thy whisper, Lord, my heart shall cheer,
"Tis I; be not afraid!"

Or, startled at some sudden blow,
If fretful thoughts I feel,
"Fear not, it is but I!" shall flow,
As balm my wounds to heal.

Nor will I quit Thy way, though foes
Some onward pass defend;
From each rough voice the watchword goes,
"Be not afraid! ... a friend!"

And oh! When judgment's trumpet clear
Awakes me from the grave,
Still in its echo may I hear,
"'Tis Christ; he comes to save."

Venerable Cardinal John Henry Newman
Verses on Various Occasions

Mary, Source of Consolation:
Three Prayers From Thomas à Kempis

If you love Jesus, come, take up his cross;
walk with the cross;
Remain near the cross;
embrace this cross and do not forsake it
until you have arrived near the One who gives glory to the cross.
If you wish in your trials, in spite of the sorrow,
to find some Consolation,
go to Mary at once virgin and mother,
to the mother who watches near the cross;
to the virgin who weeps at the foot of the cross.
All suffering will then disappear for you,
or at least will seem lighter and more bearable
compared to the griefs of the Virgin Mary.

It is to you, O Jesus, my Lord and my God,
to you, O Mary, Mother of God and my mother,
that I wish to confide my body and soul.
You alone are my hope and my help
in my troubles and in my tribulations.
Let your tenderness and your affection
sustain me everywhere!
This is my only prayer.

Extend over me, extend your arms, Mary,
 because I wish to seek my refuge in your shadow.
Say to my soul: I am your advocate, fear nothing.
 As a mother consoles her son,
 thus I shall console you, my child.
How sweet are your words, Mary,
 and how your voice consoles me, Mother!
Allow my heart to always hear it.

Thomas à Kempis
The Imitation of Mary

Abandoned on the Cross

O Jesus,... remember the grief you suffered when, naked and miserable, you hung upon the cross. You had no consolation; all your friends and relatives abandoned you. Your beloved mother, however, remained loyal to you during your agony....

I beg you, most sweet Jesus, by the sword of sorrow that pierced the soul of your mother, to have compassion on me in all my afflictions and sufferings, both physical and spiritual. Grant me consolation in every trial and especially at the hour of my death. Amen.

Attributed to St. Bridget

In Imitation of Christ

O my most compassionate Savior,
who willed, for the redemption of the world,
to carry the heavy cross upon your shoulders,
even to Mount Calvary,
grant me the grace that, following your example,
I may willingly embrace the cross
of the mortifications and trials of this world,
and bear it patiently, for love of you, even unto death.
Amen.

St. Leonard of Port Maurice
Hidden Treasure

Suffering Alone, as Did Christ

O Jesus, in that garden where the last night of your life descended upon men, and a still darker night upon your own soul, you suffered alone. Even those who loved you failed in that hour to understand you and your torture.

O my Savior, all humanity experiences that agony in the Garden of Olives, all Christian souls go through the crisis of suffering and desolation. And like you, the Christian soul is always alone in the Garden of Gethsemane, in spite of tenderness and pity sleeping close at hand. No one can cure another's grief, and sometimes those who come near only hurt the more.

Remember then, beloved Master, what that hour was to you; have pity on our weakness, and do you, who are the only Consoler, the only Heart that can share and understand, come and appease and strengthen us, and help us to make our grief into a blessing, a living sign.

Elisabeth Leseur
A Wife's Story

Meeting Christ in the Storm

Jesus, hope of suffering humanity,
our refuge and our strength,
Whose light pierces the black clouds
  that hang over our stormy sea,
enlighten our eyes so that we can direct ourselves
  toward you who are our harbor.
Guide our bark with the rudder
  of the nails of your cross,
  lest we drown in the storm.
With the arms of this cross rescue us
  from the turbulent waters
  and draw us to yourself,
our only repose, Morning Star, Sun of Justice,
for with our eyes obscured by tears,
we can catch a glimpse of you there,
  on the shores of our heavenly homeland.
Redeemed by you, we pray:
  Salvos nos fac propter nomen tuum—
  "save us for the sake of your holy name"
(St. Augustine).

St. Raphael Kalinowski
St. Raphael Kalinowski:
An Introduction to His Life and Spirituality

A Prayer of Surrender and Intercession

Lord, may you be blessed for all this suffering. I offer it all to you. Use this humble gift for my intentions, for souls, and for the church.

Accept a tithe of it in expiation of my sins and for that work of reparation which you entrust to souls who are dear to you. It is not pride, is it, Lord? Thus to call myself your friend, your chosen soul—because everywhere in my life I see the traces of your love, the divine call, the supernatural vocation.

You have made use of suffering and illness to take me entirely to yourself, first drawing me to you by your action within me. You have done *all.* And now, complete your work; make me holy insofar as you will; use me for souls, for my beloved ones, use me in your interest, for your greater glory, and let all be done in silence, heart to heart, in the privacy of my soul with you.

From the depths of my being and my misery I say to you: "Lord, what would you have me do? Speak, your servant listens; here is the servant of the Lord. I come, O Father, to do your will."

Elisabeth Leseur
A Wife's Story

One thing alone I know—that according to our need, so will be our strength. One thing I am sure of, that the more the enemy rages against us, so much more will the saints in heaven plead for us; the more fearful are our trials from the world, the more present to us will be our mother Mary, and our good patrons, and angel guardians; the more malicious are the devices of men against us, the louder cry of supplication will ascend from the bosom of the whole church to God for us. We shall not be left orphans; we shall have within us the strength of the Paraclete, promised to the church and to every member of it.

Venerable Cardinal John Henry Newman
Sermons Preached on Various Occasions

BIOGRAPHICAL INFORMATION

Albert the Great, St. (1206–80). Albert was a Dominican priest, theologian, scientist, and teacher. He was designated "the Great" due to his powerful intellect, much in evidence in his work in the areas of theology, biology, physics, geography, geology, and botany.

Alphonsus Liguori, St. (1696–1787). Founder of the Congregation of the Most Holy Redeemer (Redemptorists), St. Alphonsus devoted himself to preaching missions, especially in rural areas. He worked primarily in the region around Naples, Italy.

Ambrose, St. (340–397). As bishop of Milan, Ambrose fought against the Arian heresy then threatening the church and stood up to emperors when the occasion demanded. He was preeminently a pastor and was an effective preacher who influenced St. Augustine in his search for the truth.

Anthony Claret, St. (1807–70). The son of a weaver and a weaver himself, Claret became a priest and, after some years of pastoral and missionary work, founded the Missionary Sons of the Immaculate Heart of Mary (the Claretians). He left his native Spain and served as archbishop of Santiago, Cuba, where he survived an assassination attempt. Claret eventually returned to Spain and there helped to lead a revival of Catholicism. He was a prolific writer—he published 144 books and pamphlets—and preacher, preaching over twenty-five thousand sermons.

Augustine, St. (354–430). Augustine served as the bishop of Hippo in north Africa for over thirty years. He was a brilliant philosopher, theologian, preacher, and writer whose life and works have definitively shaped the development of the church. Over one hundred of his books and treatises, as well as two hundred letters and five hundred sermons, survive. He tells the story of his conversion in his *Confessions.*

Basil, St. (329–379). Basil is considered the founder of monasticism in the Eastern church. As bishop of Caesarea, he was known for his valiant opposition to the Arian heresy, then flourishing, and especially for his vast works of social relief on behalf of the poor and needy.

Bernard of Clairvaux, St. (1090–1153). Bernard was the abbot of the Cistercian monastic foundation at Clairvaux and helped lead the reform of medieval monastic life. He was a prolific and brilliant writer; many of his works, such as *On the Love of God* and *On the Song of Songs,* are read today. He is also known for his devotion to and sermons about Mary.

Bridget of Sweden, St. (1303–73). Bridget was a wife and mother who, upon the death of her husband, founded the religious order known as the Brigittines. She was a reformer and known for revelations and visions.

Charles de Foucauld, Venerable (1858–1916). Charles was the founder of the Little Brothers and Little Sisters of Jesus, dedicated to living and working among the poor. He himself lived a life of quiet ministry among the people of Tamanrasset, Algeria. He was shot there by rebels during a period of political turmoil.

Charles Joseph Eugene de Mazenod, St. (1782–1861). De Mazenod was bishop of Marseilles and founder of the Oblates of Mary Immaculate.

Charles of Sezze, St. (1616–70). Charles was a shepherd who wanted to become a priest. He was uneducated and therefore unable to fulfill his ambition, but instead became a lay brother at Naziano, Italy. He worked at menial jobs in monasteries around Rome and wrote several mystical works.

Claude de la Colombière, St. (1641–82). St. Claude was a Jesuit priest with a reputation as an excellent preacher. He helped promote devotion to the Sacred Heart. He served for some time as confessor to St. Margaret Mary Alacoque, who received revelations about and also promoted devotion to the Sacred Heart.

Cyprian, St. (200–58). Cyprian, bishop of Carthage during various Roman persecutions of Christians, was beheaded for his refusal to sacrifice to pagan gods. He was involved in theological controversy, particularly regarding the treatment of Christians who had lapsed from the faith when faced with persecution. He wrote theological works and pioneered Latin Christian literature.

Dorothy Day, Servant of God (1897–1980). Day cofounded the Catholic Worker Movement in New York City. She spent her adult life championing the poor and needy, opposing war, and decrying the exploitation of workers. She started *The Catholic Worker* newspaper and wrote for it for over fifty years, at the same time devoting herself to the practical aspects of the care of the destitute.

Edith Stein, St. (Sr. Teresa Benedicta of the Cross) (1891–1942). Stein was a brilliant philosopher, a Jewish convert to Catholicism, and a Carmelite nun who died at Auschwitz. The Nazis rounded up Stein (who was living in a Carmel in the Netherlands) and other Catholics of Jewish extraction in retaliation against the Dutch bishops, who had condemned the persecution of the Jews.

Elisabeth Leseur, Servant of God (1866–1914). Elisabeth offered her prayers and the physical suffering of her cancer for the conversion of her atheist husband. He found her spiritual journal after her death, read it, converted, and later became a priest. He introduced her cause for canonization to Rome.

Francis de Sales, St. (1567–1622). De Sales was the bishop of Geneva in the period following the Protestant Reformation. A brilliant, cultured man, he was nevertheless humble and had a strong pastoral instinct. He reformed his diocese, at the same time keeping up a vast correspondence with those who sought his advice. Among other works, he wrote *The Introduction to the Devout Life* to help lay people find holiness in everyday life.

Francis Libermann, Venerable (1802–52). Francis was the second founder of the Congregation of the Holy Ghost, a missionary order.

Francis of Assisi, St. (1182–1226). Francis founded the Order of Friars Minor (Franciscans). His simplicity, holiness, charisma, and emphasis on personal love for Christ helped bring about a much-needed renewal of thirteenth-century religious life.

Although born to wealth, Francis abandoned everything to live in poverty, devoting himself to the care of the sick and needy.

Frederic Ozanam, Blessed (1813–53). A married man and father, Ozanam was a popular professor of literature at the Sorbonne in France and founder of the St. Vincent de Paul Society.

Giles of Assisi, Blessed (d. 1262). One of the first followers of St. Francis, Giles was called by him his "Knight of the Round Table."

Gregory Thaumaturgus, St. (213–68). Gregory, bishop of Neocaesarea, was known for his many miracles and so was dubbed Thaumaturgus (Wonderworker). He brought many to the faith and experienced the first Marian vision on record.

Gregory the Great, Pope St. (540–604). Although his only ambition was to live as a monk, Gregory nevertheless accepted his appointment to the papacy and went on to reform the church. His writings include the *Dialogues* and *Pastoral Care.* He is closely associated with the development of liturgical music, so much so that plainsong is known as Gregorian chant.

Henry Suso, Blessed (1295–1365). Suso was a Dominican with a gift for preaching and bringing sinners to repentance. He lived and worked primarily in Germany. His *Little Book of Eternal Wisdom* is one of the most influential works in the history of mystical literature.

Jacques, Servant of God Père (1900–45). Père Jacques was a Carmelite priest and member of the French Resistance who died at the hands of the Nazis. He was arrested for sheltering three Jewish students at his school near Paris and ended up at the Mauthausen concentration camp. Louis Malle's film, *Au Revoir, Les Enfants,* tells the story of the school and the arrest of Jacques and the boys.

Jane Frances de Chantal, St. (1572–1641). Jane was happily married and the mother of seven children (four of whom survived infancy). In 1601 her husband, the Baron Christophe de Chantal, was killed in a hunting accident by a friend who mistook him for a deer. Jane devoted herself to the religious life and eventually, together with St. Francis de Sales, founded the Visitation order of nuns in France.

John XXIII, Pope Blessed (1881–1963). Known for his humor, warmth, and down-to-earth personality, Pope John XXIII convened Vatican Council II to bring about renewal in the church. His works include *Journal of a Soul* and the encyclical *Pacem in Terris.*

John Chrysostom, St. (347–407). John, the bishop of Constantinople, was known as Chrysostom—Golden Mouth—for his eloquent preaching. He was devoted to the poor and frequently urged his congregation to care for the needy. His reform of the church and opposition to government interference in church life earned him exile and early death. Many of Chrysostom's works survive and are to-the-point and relevant today.

John Eudes, St. (1601–80). Fr. Eudes founded the Congregation of Jesus and Mary, which is dedicated to preaching missions and to reforming the clergy through better seminary education.

John Eymard, St. (1811–68). Eymard founded the order of the Priests of the Most Blessed Sacrament, dedicated to maintaining perpetual adoration before the Blessed Sacrament. He also founded an order for women and numerous societies devoted to the Eucharist.

John Henry Newman, Venerable (1801–90). Newman was a prominent Anglican priest who converted to Catholicism and eventually became a cardinal. His life as a Catholic was difficult, his thinking and writing underappreciated, but his genius has been widely recognized posthumously. His writings include *Parochial and Plain Sermons, Apologia Pro Vita Sua,* and *Idea of a University.*

John of the Cross, St. (1542–91). John, cofounder of the Discalced Carmelites, helped St. Teresa of Avila in her reform of the Carmelite order. A mystic and a spiritual director, he wrote such classics as *Dark Night of the Soul* and *Spiritual Canticle.*

John Paul II, Pope (1920–). John Paul II, the first Polish pope, endured both the Nazi occupation of his homeland and, following that, life under repressive communist regimes. As archbishop and then cardinal of Cracow, he was a leader in the church's struggle against communism. Elected pope in 1978, he has consistently emphasized the global nature of the Catholic

Church, traveling widely from Africa to Japan, North and South America, Mexico, the Philippines, and elsewhere. He survived an assassination attempt in 1981. John Paul II's writings include numerous encyclicals and books including *Sign of Contradiction*, originally delivered as a series of Lenten addresses to Pope Paul VI, at his invitation.

John Vianney, St. (1786–1859). Vianney, also known as the Curé of Ars, had remarkable gifts in the confessional. He lived a life of heroic self-sacrifice in the isolated region of Ars, France, serving the legions who came to him there for spiritual direction.

Josemaría Escrivá, Blessed (1902–75). Escrivá founded Opus Dei in Spain in 1928. The worldwide organization, currently about eighty thousand strong, emphasizes the active apostolate of the laity.

Joseph Moscati, St. (1880–1927). A medical doctor in Naples, Moscati devoted himself to serving the poor.

Leo the Great, Pope St. (d. 461). Leo administered the church with unflinching courage in the face of government hostility and tumultuous times. He personally dissuaded Attila the Hun from destroying Rome but three years later endured the sack of the city by the Vandals. Pope St. Leo fought against heresy at great personal cost. Ninety-six of his sermons are extant.

Leonard of Port Maurice, St. (1676–1751). Leonard, a Franciscan, is noted for his missionary preaching and his devotion to the Stations of the Cross, the Blessed Sacrament, the Sacred Heart, and Mary.

Louis de Monfort, St. (1673–1716). De Montfort is particularly known for promoting devotion to Mary and the rosary. He was a missionary preacher and the founder of the Missionaries of the Company of Mary.

Mary Euphrasia Pelletier, St. (1796–1868). Pelletier founded the Good Shepherd Sisters in France to work with women and girls who are trapped in prostitution, abandoned, homeless, or otherwise struggling.

Mary Frances Schervier, Blessed (1819–76). Founder of the Sisters of the Poor of St. Francis, Schervier's generosity was legendary and her devotion to the poor, heroic. She herself worked primarily in Germany but in 1855 sent some of her sisters to Cincinnati, Ohio to open a hospital there.

Miguel Pro, Blessed (1891–1927). Pro, a Jesuit priest, was martyred during anti-Catholic persecutions in Mexico.

Peter Favre, Blessed (1506–46). One of the first Jesuits, Favre spent his active ministry working to heal the rift between Protestants and Catholics following the Reformation.

Philip Neri, St. (1515–95). An immensely cheerful and appealing saint, Neri evangelized Rome and founded the Oratorian order.

Raphael Kalinowski, St. (1835–1907). Kalinowski endured exile in Siberia before becoming a Discalced Carmelite in his native Poland. He helped restore the Carmel in Poland after its suppression during the Russian occupation.

Teresa of Avila, St. (1515–82). St. Teresa reformed the Carmelite order and cofounded, with St. John of the Cross, the Discalced Carmelites. She is a doctor of the church and author of such classics as *The Way of Perfection* and her autobiography.

Thérèse of Lisieux, St. (1873–97). St. Thérèse, a Carmelite nun, described her "little way" to holiness in her autobiography, *The Story of a Soul.* Her approach—living out the gospel in the mundane events of daily life—appealed to many and brought her posthumous fame. She is a doctor of the church.

Thomas à Kempis. (1380–1471). Thomas was a member of the Canons Regular at Agnietenberg and is traditionally considered the author of the devotional classic *The Imitation of Christ. The Imitation,* first circulated in 1418 and still in print, encourages Christians to achieve holiness by modeling their lives on Christ.

Vincent de Paul, St. (1580–1660). St. Vincent founded the Congregation of the Missions, dedicated to the training of the clergy and to missionary work. He was legendary in his own lifetime for his love, charisma, and devotion to the poor.

BIBLIOGRAPHY

Albert the Great, St. *On Cleaving to God.* John Richards, trans. Grand Rapids, Mich.: Christian Classics Ethereal Library at Calvin College, www.ccel.org.

Ante-Nicene Fathers, Vol V. Alexander Roberts and James Donaldson, eds. New York: Scribner's, 1919; *Vol VI*, 1925.

Augustine, St. *Confessions.* R.S. Pine-Coffin, trans. Harmondsworth, England: Penguin, 1961.

Bangert, William. *To the Other Towns: A Life of Blessed Peter Favre.* Westminister, Md.: Newman, 1959.

Basil the Great, St. *Gateway to Paradise.* Oliver Davies, ed. Tim Witherow, trans. Brooklyn, N.Y.: New City, 1991.

____. *The Fathers of the Church: St. Basil, Letters 1-185,* Agnes Clare Way, trans. New York: Fathers of the Church, 1951.

Bernoville, Gaetan. *St. Mary Euphrasia Pelletier: Foundress of the Good Shepherd Sisters.* Westminster, Md.: Newman, 1959.

Capecelatro, Alfonso. *The Life of Philip Neri, Apostle of Rome.* Thomas Alder Pope, trans. London: Burnes, Oates, Washbourne, 1926.

Carrouges, Michael. *Soldier of the Spirit: The Life of Charles de Foucauld.* Marie-Christine Hellin, trans. New York: Putnam, 1956.

Catechism of the Catholic Church. Liguori, Mo.: Liguori, 1994.

Charles of Sezze, St. *Autobiography of St. Charles of Sezze.* Leonard Perotti, trans./ed. Chicago: Franciscan Herald, 1963.

Connolly, Francis X. *Wisdom of the Saints.* New York: Pocket, 1963.

Daniel-Rops, Henri. *Monsieur Vincent: The Story of St. Vincent de Paul.* New York: Hawthorne, 1961.

Day, Dorothy. *By Little and By Little: The Selected Writings of Dorothy Day.* Robert Ellsberg, ed. New York: Alfred A. Knopf, 1983.

___. *The Long Loneliness.* New York: Doubleday by arrangement with Harper, 1959.

___. *On Pilgrimage.* Grand Rapids, Mich.: Eerdmans, 1999.

Day, Dorothy (information regarding). www.catholicworker.org.

de Breffny, Brian. *In the Steps of St. Patrick.* London: Thames and Hudson, 1982.

de Chantal, St. Jane. *The Jewels of St. Jane Frances de Chantal.* William Doheny, ed., privately circulated, 1980.

de Foucauld, Charles. *Scriptural Meditations on Faith.* Alexander Russel, trans. New York: New City, 1988.

____. *Spiritual Autobiography of Charles de Foucauld.* Jean-Francois Six, ed. © The Official Catholic Directory 2001- P.J. Kenedy and Sons, Reed Elsevier NP, New Providence, N.J. Written permission granted to publish data. All rights reserved.

de la Colombière, Bd. Claude. *The Spiritual Direction of Blessed Claude de la Colombière.* Mother M. Philip, trans. San Francisco: Ignatius, 1998.

de Montfort, St. Louis Marie. *God Alone: The Collected Writings of St. Louis Marie de Montfort*. Bay Shore, N.Y.: Montfort, 1987.

de Paul, St. Vincent. *Some Counsels of St. Vincent de Paul.* E.K. Saunders, trans. London: Heath, Cranton, Ousley, 1914.

de Sales, St. Francis. *Introduction to the Devout Life. New York: Image Books, 1972.*

____. *St. Francis de Sales: Selected Letters.* Elisabeth Stopp, trans. London: Faber and Faber, 1960.

_____. *Thy Will Be Done: Letters to Persons in the World.* Manchester, New Hampshire: Sophia Institute, 1995.

Escrivá, Blessed Josemaría. *The Way.* New York: All Saints, 1954.

Eudes, John St. *Letters and Shorter Works.* Ruth Hauser, trans. New York: P.J. Kenedy, 1948.

Favre, Pierre. *The Spiritual Writings of Pierre Favre.* Murphy, Edmond C. et al. St. Louis, Mo.: Institute of Jesuit Resources, 1996.

Field, Anne. *From Darkness to Light: What It Meant to Become a Christian in the Early Church.* Ann Arbor, Mich.: Servant, 1978.

Goepfert, Prosper. *Life of the Venerable Libermann.* Dublin: Gill, 1880.

Gregory the Great, St. *Spiritual Readings From St. Gregory the Great.* John Leinenweber, ed./trans. Cambridge, Mass.: Cowley, 1990.

Hubenig, Alfred. *Living in the Spirit's Fire: Saint Eugene de Mazenod, Founder of the Missionary Oblates of Mary Immaculate.* Toronto, Ont.: Novalis, 1995.

Jeiler, Ignatius. *Mother Frances Schervier: A Sketch of Her Life and Character.* St. Louis, Mo.: Herder, 1895.

John XXIII, Pope. *Wit and Wisdom of Good Pope John*. Henri Fesquet, ed. New York: J.P. Kenedy, 1964.

John Paul II, Pope. *Crossing the Threshold of Hope*. New York: Knopf, 1994.

___. *Salvifici Dolores*. Rome: Vatican Polyglot, 1993.

___. *Sign of Contradiction*. New York: Seabury, 1979.

Leo the Great, St. *The Binding of the Strong Man*. Anne Field, ed. Ann Arbor, Mich.: Word of Life, 1976.

Leonard of Port Maurice, St. *Hidden Treasure*. Fresno, Calif.: Academy Library Guild, 1952.

Leseur, Elisabeth. *A Wife's Story: The Journal of Elisabeth Leseur*. London: Burns, Oates, Washbourne, 1919.

_____. *My Spirit Rejoices: The Diary of a Christian Soul in an Age of Unbelief*. Manchester, N.H.: Sophia Institute, 1996.

Liguori, St. Alphonsus. *The Great Means of Salvation and of Perfection*. Eugene Grimm, ed. New York: Benzinger, 1886.

The Little Flowers of St. Francis of Assisi. Grand Rapids, Mich.: Christian Classics Ethereal Library at Calvin College, www.ccel.org.

Lozano, Juan Maria. *Mystic and Man of Action: St. Anthony Mary Claret.* Chicago: Claretian, 1977.

Marmion, Columba. *Suffering With Christ.* Raymund Thibaut, ed. Westminster, Md.: Newman, 1952.

McMullen, Richard. *Deep Down Things: Burning Love for the Poor.* New York: New City, 1995.

Mercy, Member of the Order of. *A Year With the Saints.* New York: P.J. Kenedy, 1891.

Merton, Thomas. *The Waters of Siloe.* New York: Harcourt, Brace, 1949.

Murphy, Francis J. *Père Jacques: Resplendent in Victory.* Washington, D.C.: ICS, 1998.

Newman, John Henry. *A Newman Treasury: Selections From the Prose Works of John Henry Cardinal Newman*, Charles F. Harrold, ed. New York: Longmans, Green, 1943.

____. *Meditations and Devotions.* Harrison, New York: Roman Catholic, 1893.

____. *Parochial and Plain Sermons.* London: Longmans, Green, 1907.

____. *Sermons Preached on Various Occasions.* London: Longmans, Green, 1908.

___. *Verses on Various Occasions.* London: Longmans, Green, 1903.

Newman, John Henry (writings of/information regarding). www.newmanreader.org.

Nicene and Post-Nicene Fathers, Vol. IX; X. Philip Schaff, ed. Grand Rapids, Mich.: Eerdmans, 1956.

O'Brien, Felicity. *Saints in the Making.* Dublin: Veritas, 1988.

O'Meara, Kathleen. *Frederic Ozanam: His Life and Works.* New York: Christian Press Assoc., 1876.

Philip, Mary. *A Jesuit at the English Court: A Life of Blessed Claude de la Colombière.* London: Burnes, Oates, Washbourne, 1922.

Praskiewicz, Szczepan T. *Saint Raphael Kalinowski: An Introduction to His Life and Spirituality.* Thomas Coonan, Michael Griffin, Lawrence Sullivan, trans. Washington, D.C.: ICS, 1998.

Ravier, Andre. *Saint Jeanne de Chantal.* San Francisco: Ignatius, 1989.

Saints (writings of/information regarding). www.ewtn.org.

Storey, William G., ed. *Days of the Lord, Vol. III.* New York: Herder and Herder, 1966.

Suso, Blessed Henry. *The Little Book of Eternal Wisdom.* London: Burns, Oates and Washburn, 1910.

Teresa Benedicta of the Cross, St. (Edith Stein). *The Collected Works of Blessed Edith Stein, Vol. IV: The Hidden Life: Hagiographic Essays, Meditations, and Spiritual Texts.* L. Gelber and Michael Linssen, eds. Washington, D.C.: ICS, 1992.

Teresa of Avila, St. *The Letters of Saint Teresa.* John Dalton, trans. London: Thomas Baker, 1893.

___. *The Way of Perfection.* Allison Peers, ed. Garden City, N. Y.: Image, 1964.

Tesniere, Albert. *Peter Julian Eymard: The Priest of the Eucharist.* New York: Eymard League, 1962.

Thérèse of Lisieux, St. *The Autobiography of St. Thérèse of Lisieux: The Story of a Soul.* John Beevers, trans. Garden City, N.Y.: Doubleday, 1957.

____. *The Story of a Soul: The Autobiography of St. Thérèse of Lisieux.* John Clarke, trans. Washington, D.C.: ICS, 1972.

à Kempis, Thomas. *The Imitation of Christ.* Harold C. Gardiner, ed. Garden City, N.Y.: Doubleday, 1955.

___. *The Imitation of Christ.* Croft, Aloysius and Harold Bolton, trans. Grand Rapids, Mich.: Christian Classics Ethereal Library at Calvin College, www.ccel.org.

___. *The Imitation of Mary: Extracts from the Original Works of Thomas à Kempis.* Albin Cigala, ed. Harrison, N.Y.: Roman Catholic, 1947.

Thurston, Herbert, and Donald Attwater. *Butler's Lives of the Saints, Vol. III.* Allen, Tex.: Thomas More, 1956.

VandenHeuvel, Anthony. *Titus Brandsma: A Modern Martyr for the Truth.* Welland, Ont.: The Friends of Titus Brandsma, 1989.

Van Kaam, Adrian. *A Light to the Gentiles: The Life Story of the Venerable Francis Libermann.* Milwaukee, Wis.: Bruce, 1959.

Vecchi, Juan. *Letter of the Rector Major* [Salesian Priests]: Sanctity and Martyrdom at the Dawn of the Third Millennium. July/September 1999, #368.

Vianney, St. John. *The Sermons of St. John Vianney.* www.ewtn.org.

Ward, Maisie. *Saints Who Made History: The First Five Centuries.* New York: Sheed and Ward, 1959.